10.95

The Third Act

THE THIRD ACT

Writing a Great Ending
to Your Screenplay

By Drew Yanno

continuum

NEW YORK • LONDON

2006

The Continuum International Publishing Group Inc
80 Maiden Lane, New York, NY 10038

The Continuum International Publishing Group Ltd
The Tower Building, 11 York Road, London SE1 7NX

www.continuumbooks.com

Copyright © 2006 by Drew Yanno

All rights reserved. No part of this book may be reproduced, stored in a retrieval
system, or transmitted, in any form or by any means, electronic, mechanical,
photocopying, recording, or otherwise, without the written permission of the
publishers.

Printed in the United States of America

Library of Congress Cataloging-in-Publication Data

Yanno, Drew.
  The third act : a structural approach to writing great endings / by Drew Yanno.
    p. cm.
  Includes bibliographical references and index.
  ISBN-13: 978-0-8264-1878-4 (pbk. : alk. paper)
  ISBN-10: 0-8264-1878-3 (pbk. : alk. paper)
  1. Motion picture authorship. 2. Closure (Rhetoric) I. Title.
  PN1996.Y33 2006
  808.2'3--dc22
                                                          2006016051

Contents

To Suzanne and Meghan...
for your infinite patience and support

Introduction

Imagine for a moment that at the end of the legendary film *Casablanca*, Rick allows Captain Renault to arrest Victor Laszlo while Rick and Ilsa use the much-desired exit visas to board the plane for Lisbon and, eventually, America.

Or try to picture Butch and Sundance somehow managing to shoot their way out of that small, out-of-the-way cantina and, wounded but still alive, riding off to freedom somewhere in the hills of Bolivia at the end of **Butch Cassidy and the Sundance Kid**.

Or suppose in the final moments of Barry Levinson's brilliant **Rain Man**, Charlie Babbitt succeeds in his legal battle to win custody of his autistic brother, Raymond, and the two proceed to live together in the Hollywood Hills like a couple of carefree (and rich) bachelors.

Would any of these "alternate" endings have changed your feelings about those great films?

Would they have in any way improved those already Oscar-winning hits?

Or would they have detracted from their status as "great" in the minds of all of us?

In each one of those films, we can recall exactly how they concluded, even years after first viewing them. Those images are etched in our minds forever.

In fact, it would probably not be overstating it to suggest that most of us can recall the "feeling" those endings gave us when we first viewed those films. And no doubt many would admit that they have wondered what it might have "felt" like had they ended in some other fashion.

It's likely that we concluded then and would confirm now that each of them ended exactly as they should have. Which is part of what makes them "great."

So how did they do that? How did the writers find the exact right ending for those films? How did each of those endings come about from the writers' standpoint? Did they know prior to putting fingers to keyboard that they would resolve themselves in that fashion? Did the choices the writers made along the way lead to no other conclusion? Did they know some secret that we don't?

Not likely.

Equally as unlikely is that each of them wrote that ending with the structure in mind that I am about to lay out in this book. Not consciously anyway. (In the case of Howard Koch and the Epstein brothers, the credited writers of **Casablanca**, I wasn't even alive when it was written.)

But I think it is safe to say that each of the writers of those films, as well as countless other writers of countless other "great" films, in some form or fashion, included in their writing of those endings all of the principles that you are about to read in this book.

They may not have called them the same things I do. They may not have even articulated them at all. In some instances, it may have been no more than a gifted writer's God-given talent and instinct that allowed them to produce their "great ending."

But what is instinct to some, must be taught to others. Be aware that most screenwriters have been taught how to write screenplays, either by others or through some effort of their own. Much of what we might call instinct is actually the product of learning that has been absorbed and processed and no longer requires conscious application.

If you are one of those writers whom God has blessed with pure instinct and talent, you can probably put this book down. If not, then you should keep reading.

Great endings don't happen by accident. They happen because the writer has made them happen. Oftentimes, they do so by simple trial and error (and some tireless rewrites). The writers may even credit serendipity. But I think they happen because of a time-tested structure employed by the writer either subconsciously or by that learned instinct I referred to above.

Now, you may be wondering if I am claiming to have invented something here. I'm not. What I have done is simply to articulate what already exists in many great films with great endings. It is just a new way of looking at the third and final act in a three-act story and, within it, identifying a set of principles—a structure—that seems to apply to all good third acts. In that way, it is not much different than the concept of the three-act structure itself, which has existed in cinema almost from its beginning as an art form, even though it has only been taught on a large scale for fewer than thirty years.

You may also wonder if applying these elements or principles to your writing will lead to formulaic endings. The short answer to that is no. The same concern and criticism has been leveled at writing screenplays using three-act structure ever since that paradigm was first espoused by Syd Field. The criticism does not apply there, nor should it apply here.

Want proof? Well, surely you would agree that **Good Will Hunting** does not have the same ending as **Casablanca** or **Rocky** or **Saving Private Ryan**. Yet all four of those films share the same third-act structure that I am about to set forth in this book. By the same token, those aforementioned movies are all stories told in three acts and no one would consider them to be only slight variations of one another. How can that be? How can they be both the same and different? Simple. Structure is not restrictive. It is simply instinct revealed.

It should be noted that I have developed this method of teaching the third act over the course of more than five years. I did so to make it easier for my students to understand just what is taking place in the typical third act. Thereafter, when it came time for those students themselves to begin writing, I discovered that they could use this "structure" to help them write the third act, just as they use the principles of three-act storytelling to write the entire script. After reading this book, I believe you will be able to do so as well.

Here are some things I should note before we proceed:

You can probably already tell from the title that this book does not purport to be a comprehensive screenwriting instructional manual. There are plenty of those on the market, and I suggest a number of very good ones in Appendix B at the end of this book. They are all quite useful, although, in my opinion, they don't provide what this book offers with respect to endings.

This book also does not contain any advice about how to get your script to the right producer or agent. It contains no secrets for getting people in Hollywood to read your work. There are many resources for that as well, and I offer some of those for you to consider in the same appendix.

At the same time, this book does assume that prior to reading it you have studied screenwriting at some level. If you haven't, you may want to give one of those recommended books a look before proceeding. If you would rather just plow ahead, I have included a chapter on three-act structure because it is crucial to the discussion of the structure of the third act. This may be sufficient for those of you who haven't yet studied screenwriting, but I make no promises.

Before reading any further, I strongly recommend that you watch (or watch again) the following films to assist you in understanding the examples I use in chapters 1-9:

(1) *Rocky*
(2) *Casablanca*
(3) *Witness*
(4) *Good Will Hunting*
(5) *Cast Away*

(6) *Rain Man*
(7) *Gladiator*
(8) *Saving Private Ryan*

In addition, before reading chapters 12-14, you may want to watch (or watch again) the following:

(1) *The Breakfast Club*
(2) *Diner*
(3) *The Big Chill*
(4) *Road to Perdition*
(5) *Minority Report*
(6) *Cinderella Man*
(7) *Million Dollar Baby*
(8) *Se7en*
(9) *Lost in Translation*

Whatever the level of your learning or talent, this book will help you understand the third act on a greater level and assist you in making "great" endings happen in your own writing. I can't guarantee you a great ending to your script. But I can assure you that using the methods in this book will give you a greater understanding of what you must do to get there. And I am certain that if you apply them properly, they will lead you closer to that great ending than you were before.

With that in mind, let us proceed...

Chapter One

Three-Act Structure

Beginning. Middle. End.

Aristotle said it over 2,300 years ago and it still applies today. Traditional narrative structure is a story told in three acts. Beginning. Middle. End.

The three-act structure has applied to movie writing for the better part of ninety years. In fact, many would argue that not much has changed with respect to the structure of an American screenplay over that time. Though there is some disagreement as to its origin in screenwriting instruction, Syd Field in his classic screenwriting primer, **Screenplay: The Foundations of Screen-writing** (Dell), set forth the three-act paradigm that has been pretty much followed in Hollywood from that book's publication to the present. At least two generations of screenwriters owe their careers to what Field revealed to all in his 1979 classic.

Having said all that, there are some screenwriting instructors and/or consultants who suggest a move away from the strictures of three-act writing (see, generally, **Crafty Screenwriting**, by Alex Epstein [Henry Holt, 2002]; also **Story Telling in the New Holly-wood**, by Kristin Thompson [Harvard University Press, 1999]). Still others have proposed using the structure while, at the same time, focusing on the othe parts of the craft (see David Freeman's **Beyond Structure** seminar and accompanying materials). Even the great William Goldman does not adhere strictly to the Field paradigm in terms of act/page breakdown, as witnessed by Goldman's own analysis of the second act of **Butch Cassidy and the Sundance Kid** in his classic memoir **Adventures in the Screen Trade** (Warner, 1983).

Nevertheless, many prominent screenwriting teachers have reinforced the notion of using three-act structure in the writing of American film, among them Robert McKee, David Howard, Michael Hauge, Lew Hunter, and Linda Seger. They may present differing views on what constitutes the length of an act (Hunter) or the complexity thereof (McKee), but most would probably agree that it is the dominant form of screenwriting today.

More important, Hollywood agrees. Readers doing coverage to evaluate scripts inevitably analyze those scripts with the three-act structure in mind. It is simply presumed.

For that reason, I advise my students to learn three-act structure and, at least with their early attempts at writing, I strongly urge that they apply that model to their screenplays.

Though I have no way of quantifying it, it is my guess that eighty-five percent of movies made in America follow the three-act structure that Syd Field first brought to our attention. While breaking rules is the desire of any true artist, so too is employment and a career. And eventually, even the most groundbreaking writer will someday be called upon to write a "traditional" three-act movie.

Why is that? Like Joseph Campbell's theories regarding myth, I would argue that storytelling has followed a basic three-act structure over the course of centuries and crosses just about every cultural boundary. In short, it's been that way for years, and civilized people of all nationalities have done so. I don't think movies will change that. While we all enjoy films that employ different structure from time to time, I don't believe we want to see those films exclusively or even as the predominant form of cinema storytelling.

For the purposes of this book, it is presumed that you are writing a story told in three acts. While I have provided a chapter at the end of this book about endings in films outside of the three-act paradigm, the lessons I wish to impart are definitely designed with the three-act tale in mind and work best in that form.

The model I present for the final act also presumes a single main character, as opposed to a multiprotagonist/event-based story, which is not only difficult to write, but usually has a portion of the ending built into the idea (more on this later).

If you have not read Syd Field or Robert McKee or any of the others I mentioned, I will offer here a brief primer on the three-act story. If you have read those books (and/or others) you may wish to read this chapter anyway, because it is important to bear in mind all of the aspects of traditional screenwriting when applying the principles I set forth regarding the third act.

One last note before we begin: though the topic of this book is the third act, it is my belief that a screenplay, a good one anyway, is an organic creature. One part is connected to all the others. And the removal or alteration of one of those parts has an effect, maybe small, maybe large, on the rest of the story. That is true of both scenes and the acts as well. I believe this to be particularly true of three-act stories. And, as is set forth in the following chapter, the first act and the third act are, or should be, forever joined.

Some Basics

Before talking about the three acts and structure, it may be helpful to break down screenwriting and the screenplay to its basic function and elements.

It is a widely accepted notion that a screenplay is the "blueprint" for the film that is to be eventually shot and edited. Though you will find a number of scripts for sale at your local bookstore, the screenplay is not intended to be a stand-alone art form. Its primary purpose is to be used (and most often changed) to help create another art form that is most definitely stand-alone. And collaborative. I am speaking, of course, about the finished film.

So at its essence, what is a screenplay?

Simply put, a screenplay is a series of scenes that when read together tell a story. Put another way, a screenplay (and the resultant movie) is a story told in scenes. Thus, the individual unit of a screenplay is a "scene." In turn, some of those same scenes make up each of the three acts and are the individual units contained within each.

If one were to make a visual representation of a script told in traditional three-act fashion, it would look something like this:

Act One	^ 25-30	Act Two	^ 85-90	Act Three

The numbers represent the page numbers where the breaks between the acts should occur. The ^s represent "plot points" that separate the acts. The term "plot point" was first coined by Syd Field and refers simply to a scene in which something occurs, usually affecting the main character, that takes the action and spins it around in a new direction.

One might say then that a plot point is nothing more than a scene. But is it? Surely it is a scene (and sometimes a series of scenes). At the same time, it is a specific scene that functions to separate the acts. In the theater, they close the curtains to signify the break between the acts. If there were a need to do so at the cineplex, they would close after each of these two plot points.

As an aside, Syd Field recognizes multiple plot points in any script and seems to attach greater importance to those that serve as the dividers of the acts themselves. I find this confusing and unnecessary. In a three-act screenplay, there is a need for only two plot points. Everything else is merely a scene. All scenes should act to move the plot forward, so calling them plot points seems redundant to me. Thus, for the sake of our discussion, whenever I refer to "plot points" I am referring only to those that separate the acts. Linda Seger (a fine screenwriting consultant) uses a different terminology than Field, calling these "turning points." If that makes it easier for you to understand, feel free to substitute that term.

What about the "scene" then? What is a "scene"?

A scene is a written representation of what we will see and hear on the screen. Though sound is clearly important, a scene relies on the visual above all else. After all, "movies" is short for "moving pictures," which is what film is all about.

In script form, a scene has three parts: (1) the scene heading or "slug line," (2) description and/or action, and (3) dialogue. The latter is not always necessary because we can tell the audience a great deal in a scene without dialogue. Many scenes in movies don't contain any dialogue, an important point to keep in mind in terms of storytelling on the screen. Still, the majority of scenes in a movie will contain some dialogue so I include it as one of the three elements.

By way of contrast, novelists often tell their story using a character's thoughts. Thoughts do not belong in a film, except maybe in voiceover, which is device that should be used sparingly, if at all. While a character's thoughts can be conveyed to the audience using other methods, they should *never* be written into the description contained in a scene. Only what one can see and hear (or what an actor can "play") should appear in the description.

As for how a screenwriter will reveal a character's thoughts, action and dialogue will often let the audience know what a character is thinking. However, we in the audience tend not to like it when characters tell us exactly what they are thinking. We like to participate rather than being talked to. Thus, screenwriters will often employ other methods of revealing thoughts beyond dialogue and voiceover.

Scenes are a microcosm of the screenplay itself. Just as with the three-act screenplay, each scene has a beginning, middle, and end. Note also that each scene should have at least one purpose for being in the screenplay and should only be contained in the script

if absolutely necessary for the story to be understood and appreci-
ated. Any extraneous scenes should be removed. Likewise, anything extraneous within a scene should be taken out.

Just as with the scene and the entire script, each act has a
beginning, middle, and end. Still, each act has its own purpose
and requirements. Scenes written for the first act do not belong in
the third, unless the story is told in nonlinear fashion. With that in
mind, let's take a look at each act and examine its function and
content.

Act One

In act one, the writer must "set up" the story. To do so he/she must
accomplish four things with the scenes they write for that act.

(1) The writer must **ESTABLISH** the **time** in which the story is
taking place. Is it present day? One hundred years ago? Fifty years
in the future? Locations, clothing (though writers should spend
little time on this), even language will all tell us where we are in
time in the story. Generally, the lack of any specific mention of
those things will tell the reader that the story is taking place in the
present day. Of course, there are exceptions.

The writer must also establish the **tone** of his/her story. Is it
light comedy? Drama? Horror? A writer can do this both with the
types of scenes included, as well as how those scenes are written.
This means, for the most part, what we see and what our characters do and/or say. I constantly warn my students to be careful
about the tone they set in the first few scenes, for they can unin-
tentionally create expectations regarding the story that they will
undoubtedly not be able to fulfill. This can lead to both confusion
and, possibly, resentment on the part of the reader. For instance, a
comic scene or two at the very beginning of a murder mystery or
suspense film may detract from the mood the writer ultimately
wants to convey. Of course (you guessed it), there are exceptions.

Finally, the **setting** of the story must be conveyed clearly.
Obviously, this is best accomplished by showing specific places,

both interior and exterior. However, on occasion, it may be to the advantage of the writer to mislead the reader/audience as to time and setting before ultimately revealing the true place and time. But he or she should not carry on such a ruse for very long or they will risk the same confusion and possible resentment just warned about with respect to tone.

(2) The second requirement of the writer is to **HOOK** the reader by having a scene that acts as the **inciting incident**. Robert McKee defines the inciting incident as the event that is the cause for all that follows. In doing so, this event changes the main character's life and forces him or her to move in a new direction. Usually, it is of such a nature as to prevent the main character from ignoring it and going on with their life as before. Though this can vary, the inciting incident usually occurs somewhere before page eighteen and often around the tenth page. The later it is placed in the first act, the more the writer risks losing the reader, who will be left wondering what the story "is all about."

(3) The writer must **INTRODUCE** all of the characters who will play a significant role in the story. In addition to the main character, this includes the love interest (if there is one), the villain (again, if there is one in human form) and anyone else who will be "important" in the story. By "introduce" it does not necessarily mean that we have to see the character and hear them speak. It may be enough to have them mentioned or described, so long as they (or the idea of them) does not simply pop up for the first time somewhere later in act two or three. Again, we are talking about "important" characters and not minor or secondary characters who do not play any significant part in the story.

(4) Finally, the writer must conclude the first act with the **FIRST-ACT PLOT POINT**, as described above. Again, this scene will serve to turn the action around in a new direction and lead the main character (and the audience) into the second act. In many instances, the first-act plot point is the main character's response to the inciting incident. However, there are notable exceptions to this (***Casablanca***, to name one).

Looking back, it is easy to see the beginning, middle, and end of act one.

Act Two

The second act presents the writer with his/her greatest challenge. In the Syd Field model, the second act is one-half of the entire film. The length is imposing enough, but it becomes all the more terrifying when you consider that this act does not resolve anything with the main character or the situation in which he finds himself.

To make it even more difficult, there is no simple structural design to the second act. Unlike the first act, there are no "requirements" except to keep the story moving and interesting (read: not boring). For those reasons, most writers find the second act intimidating, to say the least. But it needn't be.

The reason there is no design for the second act is that it is totally dependent upon the story and, in particular, the principal goal or desire of the main character. Put simply, whatever the main character "wants," the writer must create **OBSTACLES** that stand in the way of them achieving their goal. Moreover, these obstacles must follow logically from the situation created in the first act. They should not be lacking a nexus with all that has preceded them. Indeed, the obstacles should grow out of that which was established and "set up" in act one.

If that is not enough, these obstacles should also increase in degree of difficulty from the beginning of the second act all the way until the end of that act. If you think about it, it is simple common (movie) sense. It would make for a very boring film indeed if the most difficult challenge for the main character were to come on page forty-five and be overcome shortly thereafter.

While the number of obstacles may vary depending on the type of story, I think it is fair to say that there should be at least three obstacles that the main character must confront and overcome before they reach the end of the second act. Sometimes these obstacles are simple (i.e., "physical"). Other times, they are more internal, meaning of a psychological nature and, often, involving a relationship.

If you think of the movie *Gladiator*, in the second act Maximus starts his "career" as a gladiator by fighting in small venues against other men who harbor deadly intent, but do not quite possess the same level of skill to match. Maximus succeeds in beating a number of them and gradually moves his way up to larger arenas and more skilled opponents until he is eventually brought to Rome where he soon becomes the best of the best in what was the Roman Empire's equivalent of the major leagues.

Compare this to *Good Will Hunting*, where, in the second act, Will must wrestle with his past in both his relationship with Sean, his therapist, and Skyler, his love interest. He must also face and come to grips with his "genius" in his court-ordered meetings with Professor Lambeau. Unlike Maximus, Will confronts no physical obstacles in the second act. They are all either internal or relationship-based.

Syd Field, in his later book *The Screenwriter's Problem Solver* (Dell, 1998), proposes that there is also a "mid-point" in the second act that has some special significance. He says that it falls, not surprisingly, halfway in the story. Others agree and assign it even more importance (Thompson). Still others say there is a midpoint, but it can come later than precisely halfway through the film (see, generally, *Writing Your Screenplay*, by Lisa Dethridge [Allen & Unwin, 2003]).

I would agree that every script has a midpoint. It has to. *Something* has to happen halfway through the story. And that scene better have some significance or it doesn't belong in the script. Beyond that, however, I think it unwise to create another "important" scene that writers must first contemplate, then create, and then try to fit exactly halfway through the second act (and the entire script).

Oftentimes, the second act will also contain a scene that represents the main character's lowest point in the story. Unlike the

midpoint scene, it does not have to come halfway through the
story. If it does, that's fine. If not, that's satisfactory as well, so long
as it fits the story and the character.

If a script contains such a scene—and I maintain that it is not
always necessary—I like to refer to it as the "all is lost" moment.
Many great films contain such a scene. Some even have it as the
second-act plot point. Others have it occurring just prior to the
second-act plot point.

For example, late in the second act in **Cast Away**, Chuck (Tom
Hanks) is asleep on his not-so-sturdy raft when his only compan-
ion, Wilson the volleyball, falls overboard and drifts away. Chuck
awakens to find Wilson drifting farther from the raft. Chuck dives
in and swims to retrieve his "friend," while at the same time
clutching the rope attached to the raft so that his only means of
staying alive does not get away from him as well. In rather short
time, Chuck faces a choice: should he let go of the raft to go after
Wilson or swim back to the raft and abandon his "friend"? He
chooses the latter. And after climbing back on board, he breaks
down. He is now completely alone and adrift in the middle of the
ocean on a quickly deteriorating raft. He can't go back to the
island he has left, and there is no hope of salvation anywhere in
sight. All is lost.

Two scenes later (the next day, we presume), a ship passes
within yards of him and he is awakened from a deep sleep. He
waves to the crew and (we later learn) is rescued. End of second
act.

I should note that the second act does not have to contain a
scene representing the main character's lowest moment. Indeed, the
script may contain such a scene and have it come *after* the second-
act plot point.

For instance, in **Rocky**, our hero works himself into shape during the entire course of the second act until we finally see him race
triumphantly up the steps to the Philadelphia Art Museum, the
very same steps he struggled to climb just weeks before (at the
beginning of the second act). A second-act plot point if there ever

was one. Rocky is now ready to take on Apollo Creed. Physically anyway.

Thereafter, on the night before the fight, Rocky is unable to sleep. He leaves Adrian in bed and goes to the arena, where he takes in the atmosphere. For the first time, he sees the magnitude of what he has taken on. To make matters worse, he runs into the fight promoter who reinforces the near-impossibility of Rocky's task. Rocky then returns home and confesses to Adrian that, despite all he has done to prepare for the fight, he knows he cannot win. All is lost.

This "all is lost" moment obviously occurs after the second-act plot point. In fact, it has to occur here or he might never finish getting into shape. Note as well that this scene also serves to solidify Rocky's main desire, which up to this point is generally to prove that he is not a "tomato." In this scene, Rocky tells Adrian that he doesn't care if he wins, he only wants to "go the distance," something no other fighter has ever done against Creed. There is no way the scene could have come sooner.

Another example of the "all is lost" scene occurring *after* the second-act plot point is in **Gladiator**. Late in the second act, Maximus is reunited with Cicero, his former adjutant, who he enlists to help him escape so that he can round up his old army and take on Commodus in what would shape up to be a rousing battle. In the second-act plot point, Maximus meets with the Roman senator Gracchus and Lucilla, the emperor's sister, and in that meeting Maximus agrees to join their plot to overthrow the emperor.

However, the emperor soon learns of the plot and, in the course of Maximus's planned escape, Cicero is killed and Maximus is captured. There will be no escape, no rounding up of the army, and no assault on the city of Rome. Maximus is taken back to the gladiator's quarters and put under lock and key. All is lost.

Whether the "all is lost" moment occurs before or after the second-act plot point, or not at all, the second act must conclude with a plot point that takes the action and spins it around into the third act. What this scene consists of is entirely dependent on the story and, as with those second-act obstacles, must grow out of all that has preceded it.

Which brings us to the subject of this book.

The Third Act

Syd Field sums up the third act in one word: resolution.

That is not all he says about it, of course. But it is the gist of his theory. The third act "resolves the story," he says. And he's right. It does.

Michael Hauge refers to the third act as simply "resolve." As in "the goal of Act 3 is to resolve everything, particularly the outer motivation and conflict for the hero." And right he is.

Lew Hunter says the third act is best defined as "the conclusion." Hard to argue with that. Like "resolution," "conclusion" seems to sum up things nicely. He goes on to say that the third act is the easiest to dissect (I agree). He further states that the third act has a beginning, middle, and end. True. But so does life, which is neither a screenplay nor a movie.

Compare these authors' theories to Robert McKee, who has his own views on the third act and endings. For example, he says "resolution" is all that follows the "climax." McKee uses the term "climax" the way Field uses "resolution." And McKee uses the term "resolution" the way others might use "denouement." (By the way, Linda Seger uses the same terminology as McKee.)

No wonder writers struggle to write "good" scripts.

Let me say this: all those guys are right.

Let me say this as well: they are all wrong.

There. Does that clear things up?

The easy way out of this is to say that whatever works for you, the writer, is "right." If that is Hunter or Hauge or McKee or none of them, then that's fine. If it's something you have come up with on your own, go for it.

But I believe there is something more at work in the third act than just a few simple words. What I offer you in this book is my own take on it, using some new and different terms and concepts. It is really just another way of looking at the third act, but with the specific aim of breaking it down into manageable pieces so as to help you actually write it. I believe you will find it easy to understand and simple to apply, so long as you are writing a three-act story.

Built into this theory is some flexibility, but also some requirements that your third act cannot survive without. It may seem like common sense to you after you read it. If so, that's good. All the easier to employ.

However, before we go on, it's important for us to take another look back at that first act. And reveal its connection to the third...

Chapter Two

The First Act–Third Act Connection

Q uestion. Answer.
That's it, in a nutshell.
In a traditional three-act screenplay, the writer should, in some form or fashion, raise a question by the end of the first act that the reader/audience will look to have answered at the end of the script.

In the preceding chapter, I outlined the four requirements that the writer must fulfill in writing their first act. Nowhere in that list did I mention a question of any sort. And yet, if the writer does his or her job, a question will naturally arise.

Again, we are talking about traditional three-act structure and a single main character. The same is most likely true as well with a dual-protagonist story such as **Butch Cassidy and the Sundance Kid** or **Thelma & Louise**, but not likely with a multiprotagonist, event-based story, the reasons for which I will explain in a later chapter.

So how does this question come about? Where does it come from? Well, let's start with some basics.

The best definition I have ever heard for a "good" movie idea (to be told in three acts) is this:

Somebody wants something badly and goes after it against great odds.

I wish I could take credit for that definition, but it is, if not a direct quote from someone else, at least a paraphrasing of a very similar notion.

On the surface, this statement is quite simple. But often, so too are the best movie ideas. That is the beauty of this definition.

Think about all that this simple phrase contains.

First, the word "somebody." Notice it's not "lots of people." Not "two people." Not "an entire nation." Somebody. One person. A single main character.

Second, this somebody "wants something badly." "Wants" implies desire. We want our single main character to have an external (and often an internal) desire. We as human beings want things all the time. We want to go to the movies, for instance. And when we go to the movies, we want to see a good story. A good story almost always is one in which "somebody wants something."

It is important to note that "something" is used here to mean something specific. It does not mean "many things." Nor does it mean some yet-to-be-chosen object, though the word "something" often has that connotation, as in something/anything. Used here, it means some "thing." Some specific "thing."

And note also that this "want" is not lukewarm. It is not a weak desire. The "thing" is wanted "badly." Which means our "somebody" must have it or face some considerable consequence by not obtaining or achieving it. Common sense. After all, who cares if "somebody" wants "something" but can easily live without it and not care one way or the other if it becomes his or hers?

The second half of the definition tells us more. Our "somebody" not only wants this "thing" badly, but "goes after it." In other words, they don't wait for it to come to them. They don't rely on others to do the dirty work for them. They go after it. "Go" is an active verb. It implies action. Action implies movement. Movement is what we want because our script is the blueprint for making a "moving picture."

"Goes after it" also implies starting in one place and moving to some other place or places. Which implies direction. Movies have a direction to them. They start one place and end somewhere else, even if they are framed. Because if they do come back to the same place, as in a "framed" story, they only do so after having been elsewhere.

Of course, "goes after it" does not have to mean literally moves from one place to another. It can be metaphorical. It can mean both doing and avoiding things in order to achieve the object of their desire, though obviously action is preferred in "moving pictures." There are lots of ways to get what one wants without actually running a race or taking a literal journey.

Finally, our "somebody" not only wants this "something badly" and "goes after it," but must also do so "against great odds." In other words, it won't be easy. In fact, the odds are stacked against them. Not in some small way, but significantly so. Chances are they won't make it. If you had to bet, you'd bet against them obtaining "it." "Against great odds" also implies resistance. Resistance creates friction. Friction is conflict. Conflict means obstacles. Hey, that's our second act!

In fact, you can easily break down this definition into the three acts.

Act One

"Somebody wants something badly." Four simple words. Taken together they pretty much mean "set up," don't they? Person. Desire. Object. Urgency. Much of what the writer needs to put in the first act is contained in those four words.

Act Two

"And goes after it against great odds." Seven words this time. Those first four clearly setting our "person" on a journey. What kind of journey? Judging from those last three words, a dangerous one perhaps. Certainly not an easy one. Things will stand in their way. Maybe even three or more things, those things taking the form of obstacles. Probably each one getting harder than the one before it.

Act Three

Oops. We're out of words. Hey, what happened to our third act?!

Don't worry. It's there. Not in words, maybe. But implicitly. After all, what are we left with after our "somebody" goes after the "thing" they want "badly" against those "great odds"?

Simple. A question. A question that is raised by all those words combined: will they get it?!

Hey, they want it badly. It's likely that they won't get it, or at least the odds are stacked against them. But don't stop now! Keep going! Let me see! Do they get it?!

And that's your movie. A question and an answer.

The question is raised in act one. Answered in act three. Simple. Common sense. But you'd be surprised at how many novice screenwriters write their script and never answer the question they raised in the first act. Oh, I don't mean they fail to provide some sort of ending. They do. After all, they have to stop writing. It's just that they don't provide an ending that answers the question *they* raised in the first place.

Chances are, because they do end their script, they may answer some other question. They may resolve *something*. But oftentimes, beginning screenwriters lose sight of what they started out to do in the first place.

An even more common mistake of beginning screenwriters is failing to raise a coherent, easy to figure out question at the end of the first act. In other words, they set up *something*. Or try to at least. They may show us the setting and time. They may establish the tone and introduce all the important characters. They may even give us an inciting incident that changes life for their main character in an irrevocable fashion. But then somewhere in the second act they take a wrong turn and send the main character off seeking something else. Or worse, seeking nothing at all and merely reacting to events outside their control.

From there, they may come to some sort of conclusion. But as to *what* often remains a great mystery. If it does not relate to what we read in the first act, it will make the story seem disjointed and unresolved. And that is death to a screenplay (and movie).

Let's look at some examples of first-act questions and third-act answers.

(1) *Saving Private Ryan*

As good an idea for a movie as there has ever been.

"Somebody (Captain Miller) wants something badly (Private Ryan) and goes after it against great odds (behind enemy lines with German troops waiting at every turn)."

You will recall that in the first act Captain Miller is given a "tough" assignment, "straight from the top": find and bring back Private James Ryan. Obviously, the question is then firmly planted in our minds. Will Captain Miller "save" Private Ryan?

In act three we get our answer: yes. But at a price. Captain Miller loses his life in the process, making the ultimate sacrifice in a war that was all about American men making sacrifices.

Simple question. Simple answer.

(2) *Chinatown*

A detective story. Ready-made for question and answer.

Jake Gittes finds himself the victim of a "setup" by the fake Mrs. Mulwray in the first act and when the real Mrs. Mulwray shows up he nearly has his license taken away. Naturally, he wants to find out who did this to him and why. The question we are left with is, will he find out who set him up and why?

The answer? Yes. In the third act, Gittes learns that Noah Cross did so in order to find his daughter/granddaughter. But once again, the answer comes with a price. Evelyn Mulwray, the woman Gittes comes to know and perhaps fall in love with, gets shot and dies at the end. Gittes has his answer, but not much else. Hardly a happy ending. But a clear answer to our question.

(3) *Gladiator*

Sometime early in the first act, Marcus Aurelius, the Roman Emperor, asks Maximus to lead Rome, during a transition, time from imperial rule back to a republic. Maximus tells the Emperor he just wants to return home to his family, but he will think about it and give him an answer.

However, before Maximus can do so, the emperor's jealous son, Commodus, kills his father so that he may ascend to the throne. Maximus is then betrayed by Commodus and ordered killed. But somehow Maximus fashions an escape and returns home only to find that his wife and child have been slaughtered. A short time later, he is captured and forced to become a gladiator. Hey, wait a minute. What the hell is our question?

One could say that the question is: will Maximus help to turn Rome into a republic? But given all that has happened to him, this seems pretty far from our minds. And his.

One might also say that the question is, will Maximus get revenge?

However, revenge never seems to be Maximus's ultimate desire. He tells Marcus Aurelius (and us) that he simply wants to go home to his family. That is Maximus's stated desire. But he can't get that now. (Or can he?)

In the third act, we get an answer to both the revenge question and the one involving the republic when Maximus kills Commodus on the floor of the Colosseum, allowing for the republic to take over governing the Roman people. However, Maximus is mortally wounded in the process.

So what happens? As he dies, we see Maximus reuniting with his family (in the afterlife, we presume) in that same place where he found them dead. A great ending. What seemed like a forgotten question (will he help Rome transform into a republic) and an unattainable desire (will he get to return to his family) both get answered in the affirmative in the third act. In very satisfying fashion.

(4) *Rain Man*

In the first act, Charlie Babbitt learns in rapid succession that his estranged father has died, that he (Charlie) has an older brother he never knew, that this brother is autistic, and that his father has left nearly all of his considerable estate in a trust to be overseen by Doctor Bruner for the care of this autistic brother.

So what does Charlie do? He kidnaps his brother so that he can gain custody over him, which will mean he (Charlie) might gain some control over the money in his father's estate. Oh, and Charlie just happens to need that money to make repairs to some very expensive cars that he has imported and on which he will lose an awful lot of his own money if he is unable to do so.

The question raised at the end of act one is simple: will Charlie gain custody of his brother Raymond so that he can get at that money?

The answer at the end of act three: no. Raymond is going back to Wallbrook with Doctor Bruner. And Charlie doesn't get the money. Simple question. Simple answer.

Hey wait. That means the main character wanted something badly and went after it and didn't get it. Is that okay?

You bet. In fact, it's more than okay. In this movie, it turns out to be a very good thing. (But more on *that* in a later chapter.)

(5) *Good Will Hunting*

In the first act, Will solves a seemingly unanswerable math problem while working as a janitor at MIT. He also gets arrested for assault and, to avoid going to prison, is forced to meet with a therapist about controlling his anger. And, oh yeah, Will has to meet with the math professor who has been looking for him ever since he solved the unanswerable problem put on the board by that very same professor.

So what's our question at the end of the first act?

Well, I suppose it's simple: what will happen to Will? Will he use his gifts (superior intelligence) to become something more than a janitor?

But is that what Will wants?

Hardly. So what does Will want? Do we know after the first act?

Nope.

However, sometime late in the second act Will has a discussion on the construction site with his best friend, Chuck (Ben Affleck). In that conversation, we learn that Chuck thinks Will should use his genius, that it is his ticket out of South Boston, and that he'd be a fool not to do so. But Will tells Chuck (and us) that he doesn't want to do any such thing. Will says he wants to stay right there in South Boston for the rest of his life and hang out with Chuck and his other friends.

Suddenly, it dawns on us. Of course! His friends are the only "family" Will has ever known. As Sean tells him (and us) they'd lay down in traffic for him, unlike the foster families Will was forced to live with growing up. Why would he ever want to leave those friends?

Now, did Will want this back in the first act? I'm sure he did. Except we didn't know that then. But we do now, late in the second act.

So how about our third act? Do we get an answer to the question raised at the end of the first act?

Yes. Will is going to use his genius and become something more than a janitor. Technically, he never actually takes the job. But by telling Sean he was going to, he tells us that he will take some such job eventually.

But what about what our main character wants? To stay in South Boston with his friends? Does he get it?

No. Of course not. He's leaving! He's off to California to find Skyler at Stanford! He's not going to stay in South Boston for the rest of his life!

The lesson here is that sometimes the question raised at the end of the first act is not the same as what our main character wants. And when that happens, it is the writer's responsibility to answer *both* questions in the third act.

Some writers would answer the question raised at the end of the first act without ever answering the later question about what the main character wants. In fact, they may have never told us what the main character wants. Which is why the scene at the construction site in **Good Will Hunting** is so important. We learn what Will has always wanted and relate it back to the first act *in our minds*. And thus it must be answered.

If Will's want was never clearly articulated and answered, we still would have had a somewhat complete story. We would have had an answer to the question raised in the first act (what will happen to Will?). We just wouldn't have had as good a movie. Because knowing what Will wants is important for us to completely understand and appreciate his actions at the end of the movie.

Notice that this is different than in **Gladiator**, where, similarly, the question raised at the end of the first act (will Maximus fulfill Marcus Aurelius's wish and help turn Rome into a republic?) is not the same as the want that the main character articulates (to get home to his family). However, in **Gladiator** we abandon the question involving our character's articulated desire because his family is dead and gone. And we almost forget the question of Rome becoming a republic because of the struggles facing Maximus. Instead, we focus on the one involving revenge.

But like **Good Will Hunting**, the writer still answers both. And surprises us in doing so. (More on *that* in a late chapter.)

The lesson then is simple: in the third act, you must always answer the question raised at the end of the first act. And if the question raised at the end of the first act does not coincide with your main character's stated desire, you must make sure the reader (audience) finds out, eventually, what your main character wants. And then, in your third act, you must answer that as well.

Obviously, not all stories require the answering of two questions. Many times the main character's desire will be the same as the question raised at the end of the first act. But on those occasions when the story separates the two, you must answer both.

Question. Answer.

That's it. That's your first act–third act connection. No more. No less.

Chapter Three

The Structure of the Third Act

Okay. So the objective of the screenwriter is to raise a question in the first act and answer it in the third, along with answering the question of the main character's desire, if that is a separate question.

How do you do that?

Well, much of it is dependent upon the story you choose to write. And some of it is just plain common sense. But a great deal of it is wide open. A wrong choice here or there and your ending will turn out badly. And that is the lasting impression your script will leave in the mind of the reader.

One way to avoid this is to look at the structure of the typical third act. Regardless of the type of story, there are at least four common elements to every third act. On the surface, they may seem simple and self-evident. And yet writers—including rich, famous, credited writers—sometimes make the mistake of not paying careful enough attention to each of these elements.

In addition, there is often a fifth element that is used by the writer in the third act. Not every script demands this fifth element. But when the circumstances call for it, the inclusion of this scene or scenes will make a huge difference in how your ending is received.

So what are these elements?

The four essential parts to every third act are as follows:

(1) The setup of the final battle
(2) The final battle
(3) The outcome of the final battle
(4) The denouement

The optional fifth element is something I call "the bridge."

Notice that three of these elements involve something called "the final battle." Once again, I didn't invent the concept. Linda Seger makes mention of something similar in her fine book *Making a Good Script Great*. And Michael Hauge refers to something he calls the "final confrontation" in his equally fine *Writing Screenplays That Sell*. Same thing, different words.

The notion of a "final battle" is not new or unique. But breaking down the structure of the third act into elements surrounding that notion has not yet been explored. Still, every writer who has written a screenplay in three acts for a successful and well-received film has most likely included the four elements I have listed above.

If successful writers already do this, why is it important to even talk about?

Because every unsuccessful writer of a three-act script most likely has failed to include one or more of those four elements in his or her third act. Or if they did include them, they may have neglected to properly set up the final battle or tailor it and its outcome to the question that was raised at the end of their first act.

Remember our second act? That long, imposing, difficult to write second act? What was that all about again?

Obstacles. Mounting obstacles. Obstacles that grow in difficulty until our main character reaches the point in the story where the second-act plot point spins it around in a new direction.

Well, when that happens, what is there waiting for our main character? Quite simply, another obstacle! Only this obstacle is far more difficult than any they faced in act two. If it's not, then it isn't worth reading/watching any more. If our main character has already faced their biggest challenge somewhere in the second act, everything after that is a letdown.

In a three-act script, the biggest obstacle for our main character must come right before the end. It should be the mother of all obstacles. Often, if we writers are doing our job right, it's the thing our main character has been fearing the most. And just as often, it couldn't come at a worse time. The more inconvenient, the better. As in: now we'll really get to see what he or she is made of. After all, isn't that why we watch movies in the first place?

In the next five chapters, we will explore each of these elements of the third act in greater detail. But before we do that, let's examine how we go about creating that huge, seemingly insurmountable obstacle for our main character in the third act.

I mentioned earlier that the obstacle could be our character's biggest fear. In *Jaws*, for instance, Sheriff Martin Brody fears the water more than anything, maybe even more than that shark. So what becomes Brody's biggest obstacle as we head into the third act?

Early on in the third act, we learn that the boat Brody is on is not going to provide adequate protection from the shark for him and Quint and Hooper. To make matters worse, Quint destroys the radio so that they cannot even place a call for help. So when that boat begins to sink, there is only one place for Brody to go. You guessed it: into the water.

As we know by now, Brody hates the water. But he's also developed a pretty good fear of that two-ton shark. That's a pretty good combination—Brody going into the water, with the shark.

Instead of our main character's biggest fear, sometimes the obstacle that they are to face in the third act is something that has been looming in the distance and can no longer be avoided. At the end of the first act in *Rocky*, our hero accepts the challenge to fight Apollo Creed. The fight is already scheduled. The day is going to come. He knows it and we know it. And so it must come. And we know this obstacle will be a lot more difficult than running up the steps of the Philadelphia Art Museum or punching the sides of beef at the meat-packing plant where Paulie works.

In stories like this, the writer's choice is simple. But in that case, the lead-up to the obstacle and the choreography thereof often become the greater challenge for the writer.

But what about something like *Saving Private Ryan*? Here the choices facing Robert Rodat (the screenwriter) were many and varied. Captain Miller had no "biggest fear." Heck, he was living his biggest fear every day he was in uniform. So how does the writer make a choice in a story like this?

William Goldman, writing about this very thing in *The Big Picture* (Applause, 2000), claimed that he was disappointed with the third act of *Saving Private Ryan*. He said that once Miller found Ryan, he thought they were going to turn around and head back and really face some obstacles.

Now, I'm not one to disagree with Mr. Goldman. Not often anyway. He is an icon whom I admire greatly. (My students would probably use the word "idolize.") In fact, when I first read Goldman's take on this, I agreed. But over time, I switched sides, and now believe that Rodat and Spielberg made an excellent choice to have Miller and his men stay and help Ryan and his makeshift platoon defend the bridge.

Why? Well, to take the approach Goldman suggested would have meant a third act with more than one obstacle. And those obstacles would have had to increase in intensity. Which is a lot like a second act. Which means Goldman's proposed third act would be a *second* second act.

In some ways I can understand Goldman's suggestion. After all, the third act in *Butch Cassidy* is really a second second act and a very short third act all rolled into one. But that is hard to pull off if your name isn't William Goldman.

In *Private Ryan*, the choices facing Rodat and Spielberg were many. But all those choices had to involve the German forces behind whose lines the Americans were, and who outnumbered the American troops by a considerable margin.

So where to take Miller and his men in the third act? Have them retrace their steps? No. We'd already been there. That violates one of the basic rules of screenwriting (and moviemaking): don't repeat yourself. And they couldn't very well keep going to Berlin. So what does that leave?

Defend the bridge. Ryan's refusal to leave his men makes sense to us. So does their order to defend the bridge at all cost. And so does Miller's decision to stay and help. An excellent choice by the filmmakers. (More on this in the next five chapters.)

The writers of **Gladiator** faced a similar problem. You'll recall that the second-act plot point was Maximus joining with Gracchus and the emperor's sister to arrange for Maximus to escape and return with his army and defeat Commodus, thereby restoring the republic just as Marcus Aurelius had requested in the beginning of the first act. Personally, I was looking forward to this. That would have made for one heck of a final battle, I thought. So I was rather disappointed when Commodus thwarted Maximus's plan and killed Cicero and arrested Gracchus. No escape. No round-up. No marching back to Rome. No rousing battle of two armies.

Screenwriting is all about choices. And the writers of **Gladiator** made a different choice. And, upon further examination, they were probably correct.

In order for Maximus to round up his army, prepare for a major invasion, and attack Rome, it would have taken up some considerable screen time. Not only that, but Maximus would have had to eventually take on Commodus one-on-one anyway. That's just how it works. Our hero must take on and defeat the villain. It can't be left up to some other character. It can't be a stray arrow or the tip of a sword wielded by someone other than the main character that causes the defeat of the villain. (Unless the main character sets in motion the events that inexorably cause such a conclusion.) It must be face-to-face, with the hero clearly overmatched. Think Apollo Creed versus Rocky Balboa.

If Maximus had assembled his army and invaded Rome, the writers still would have had to put him in a position where he was

one-on-one with Commodus, without any help from his lieu-
tenants or any others in his army. Which means a lot of activity to
get where they got anyway.

And with whom would the army have fought up until that
point? Faceless, nameless soldiers? Other than Commodus, there
were no other villains who would be worthy opponents for Maximus and his army.

Upon further analysis, the writers made a good choice. Skip all
the extracurricular activity and get right to the one-on-one battle
between Commodus and Maximus.

But wait. Didn't I say the main character had to be overmatched? How could Commodus overmatch Maximus, the MVP
of the gladiator league, in a one-on-one battle? Well, if you recall,
this was accomplished quite simply and in keeping with the character of Commodus. He cheated. He stabbed Maximus in the
back. Literally. Just prior to the fight. Not enough to kill him
immediately, but enough to significantly inhibit his fighting ability—so much so that Maximus was literally bleeding to death as
he tangled with Commodus. And he still won!

The lesson in all of this is that whenever your final obstacle is
not an inevitable event, such as the fight in **Rocky**, you must
somehow figure out how to get your hero face-to-face with his
antagonist. And for maximum impact, you must have the hero be
overmatched. If you have created a good movie villain, that
should already be the case. If not, some clever writing, such as that
in **Gladiator**, must be employed.

And if there is no singular, human villain as in **Private Ryan**,
your choice must make both logical and cinematic sense. And it
must put your hero in a place where they are at maximum risk.
Chief Brody in the water with the shark is a good example.

Now, this is all well and good when one is talking about action
movies or even movies where there is a clear "villain." But what
about in "character pieces"? What about when the main character
isn't at risk physically? How does one get their character to face
their greatest obstacle in the third act?

In those instances, the choices become more difficult. Or do they?

We'll talk more about this when we discuss "the final battle." But for now, let's turn our attention to how we "set up" that final confrontation.

Chapter Four

Setup of the Final Battle

L ike a good trial lawyer getting ready for an upcoming trial, the key to creating a great ending is preparation.

More specifically, before you get to the final battle, you must prepare for or "set up" the one-on-one battle that will take place between your main character and the antagonist. Or, if there is no villain in human form, you must arrange for the main character to face his or her greatest obstacle. As with the entire three-act screenplay, your final battle must be properly "set up" in order for the ending to achieve maximum impact.

Don't be confused by my use of the term "preparation." When I talk about "preparing" for the final battle, I am talking about the job of you as the writer. Preparing for the final battle is not something the main character does. Not in every instance anyway. And never all by himself or herself.

Sometimes the main character will take steps to prepare for the final battle, or at least some aspects of it. After all, we want our main character to "act" and not just "react." But that just means that they will have a hand in "preparing" for the final battle. They will play a part in the preparation. But even in instances where our main character hatches the entire "plan" leading to the final battle, it is the writer's job to use the main character and any others who might be necessary to properly "set up" the final battle.

In fact, the writer can and should use everything and everyone available to him or her to make certain that the most effective final battle is ready to be staged. That may include weather and any other events outside the control of any of the characters. The more complications, the better.

Why? No matter how much preparation the main character may take, we as moviegoers have come to expect that things will go awry. Indeed, we love it when that happens in films. As in war, plans often go out the window the minute the cinematic final battle starts. And in the case of the villain (should there be one), he or she should act in ways that are unexpected by the main character.

So how does a writer go about "preparing" for the final battle. Again, it is almost totally story-dependent. There is no maximum amount of time (or pages) to be spent on this. Some stories will require longer "preparation" than others.

Likewise, there is no strict requirement that the main character be involved in the preparation. Sometimes they won't be, while other characters will. However, most times it will be a combination.

Let's look at some examples from some popular and successful films to see how those final battles were "set up":

(1) *Saving Private Ryan*

Most would agree that the second-act plot point in **Saving Private Ryan** occurs when Private Ryan refuses to leave the other men in his makeshift platoon to go back with Captain Miller so that he can be shipped home. At that point, Captain Miller must make a choice. He can order Ryan to accompany him. He can even take him into custody and bring him along against his will. Instead, Miller consults with his sergeant (Mike) and decides to stay and help defend the bridge.

Now act three can begin. So how does the writer "prepare" for the upcoming final battle?

Among other things, writer Robert Rodat uses his main character (Captain Miller) to coordinate a plan for defending the bridge. Given Miller's rank, this makes perfect sense. However, Rodat also uses the other characters to inventory their resources and gather ammunition. Together, they select spots where various members of the group will be stationed when the battle begins. They even make "bombs" out of socks and axle grease.

But they also sit and talk and listen to a recording and reminisce. And that has nothing to do with the coming battle. It is character revealing. A bit of a "campfire" scene. A chance for us to catch our breath before the action starts. Maybe an opportunity to consider the magnitude of what is about to occur. But from the writer's standpoint, this scene is "preparation" for the final battle as much as the bomb making.

Think about it. If the characters were to go right from the nuts and bolts of actually preparing for the full-blown battle, we might not appreciate all that is at stake. Remember, these are ordinary men in extraordinary circumstances. Which is a phrase that describes that entire war. Which is the whole point of the film. We need a reminder of that before the battle beings.

But what about the "villain"? Does the villain play any role in "preparing" for this upcoming battle? Well, recall that there is no one villain in this film. Instead, the entire German army, or at least the portion in France at that time, represents the opposing force for Captain Miller in his attempt to save Private Ryan. And they must be preparing as well. They aren't going to just show up and happen upon this bridge. Heck, we've been told they're coming. And we can tell by the strength and coordination of their attack that it must have been planned. Yet the writer does not show us any of that.

Why not? Because it did not serve the story. We already know that Miller and the rest are vastly outnumbered. We already know that they will face a force that is far superior in strength and firepower. The "sock bombs" alone tell us that. There is no need to show the German army before the battle. Better that we take in the magnitude of their forces for the first time when they appear. From a dramatic standpoint, it is far better that we learn at the same time as Miller and his men just how bad the situation is. No need for superior knowledge here.

Compare this to:

(2) *Witness*

Our hero, John Book, is still on the farm in Amish country when our second-act plot point occurs. In this film, it is almost academic to designate which individual scene actually serves as the plot point. They are all so crucial to the story and bring us to the same spot that it simply serves no purpose to single out any one scene as the actual plot point.

Still, let's consider them in order. Book goes to town with Eli and makes a phone call to the Philadelphia police department hoping to talk with his partner, Carter. He quickly learns that Carter is dead, having died "in the line of duty." Book knows it was no such thing. He knows that his supervisor, Paul Schaeffer, along with corrupt cops McFee and Fergie had to have killed Carter.

So what does Book do next? He calls Schaeffer at home and threatens to kill him, managing to throw quite a scare into his superior, the obvious villain of this story. Then, still seething, Book rides in the buggy with Eli and they encounter some local youths who are harassing Hochleitner and some of the other Amish.

Book gets out of the buggy and approaches the youths. After they mistake Book for one of the nonviolent Amish, Book proceeds to kick the tar out of them. In doing so, he is witnessed by one of the locals, who then informs the sheriff who Schaeffer had spoken with over the phone earlier in the second act when Schaeffer was trying to locate Book.

That night, Book helps Eli repair the birdhouse he knocked down upon his arrival. Eli then enters the kitchen and tells Rachel that Book will be leaving in the morning. After Eli retires to bed (presumably), Rachel hurries out to Book in that open field where they embrace and kiss.

Which one of those is the plot point? You pick. They are all so connected and vital to the story that they must be included in the script/film. And together they all lead to the same unmistakable conclusion: Book can no longer stay hidden on the farm. He has to leave. End of second act. On to the third.

Now the writers had several choices facing them here. Certainly, they could have had Book drive back to Philadelphia where he could have made good on his threat to Schaeffer. The problem? It would be Book against three, and maybe many more, corrupt police officers. That's good in terms of drama, as pointed out earlier. But is it realistic? What would Book's plan be? How would the writers "prepare" for that? And how to get Schaeffer and Book into the desired one-on-one confrontation on Schaeffer's home turf?

As logical as Book's return might seem to be on the surface, it makes no sense upon close examination. Instead, the writers choose to have the villain take action. The net result being that the preparation for the final battle in this film is almost entirely the work of the villain and his cohorts!

Once again, as in **Saving Private Ryan**, obvious off-screen action has taken place. Schaeffer and McFee and Fergie have received word from the Lancaster County sheriff. They have gotten together (probably in Philadelphia) and made a plan. They have met up very early that morning and have driven from Philadelphia to Lancaster. None of which we see.

All that we see is the car peeking over the crest of the hill, just before dawn. It disappears and parks out of sight of the farmhouse. Then Schaeffer and the other two get out, grab weapons and ammunition, and make the slow walk down to the farm.

Notice that their "plan" was to surprise Book and the others by arriving before dawn. Apparently, they are not wise to the ways of the Amish, because we have seen that the Amish are up and do their chores long before dawn ("Four-thirty! Time for milking!").

Not one bit of the preparation for this final battle is the work of John Book. In fact, until Schaeffer and the others crash through the kitchen door, Book is not even aware that there will be a battle that day. Indeed, his plan, if he has one, is to get in the car and drive back to Philadelphia sometime that morning.

If you select any one of the scenes prior to Book and Eli's return to the farm after their fateful day in town as the second-act plot point, then everything that occurs that night is preparation for the final battle. But again, that is the work of the writers and not Book. He is completely unaware of the battle that will come the next morning. Quite simply, other than healing, Book does nothing to prepare for this final battle.

And it works. Because in this story, as opposed to **Saving Private Ryan**, it is far superior to have both the audience and Book unaware of the arrival of Schaeffer and the others. There is no need for the anticipation of their arrival, as in **Saving Private Ryan**. In that case, such anticipation serves the story better than surprise.

(3) *Rocky*

In **Rocky**, even more than in **Saving Private Ryan**, we know what's coming. From the time Rocky accepts the promoter's offer to fight Apollo Creed, we know the fight will take place. And our main character certainly prepares for the final battle. Except that he does so *in the second act*.

Once Rocky races up the steps to the Philadelphia Museum of Art, he has done all he can to prepare for the fight. In fact, that is our second-act plot point. So what happens next?

As we noted in chapter 1, the night before the fight, Rocky is unable to sleep. He goes to the arena and runs into the promoter. Rocky takes in the magnitude of what he is about to do. He then returns to his little apartment where he confesses to Adrian that he cannot win. Instead, he simply wishes to "go the distance." Preparation? By the writer certainly. But no one would call what Rocky does in those scenes "preparation."

What next? On the night of the fight, we see the fighters in their respective locker rooms. Rocky has a final conversation with Adrian before leaving the room. The fighters then enter the arena separately, Rocky without much fanfare, Apollo like the champion he is. Then we have the introductions and the brief recitation of the rules. All of it is preparation, but none of it by the main character. In fact, it is largely the work of other characters. Though all of it is really the work of the writer.

Unlike John Book, our main character is aware of what is about to take place. But like John Book, the events leading up to the final battle are largely out of his hands. Instead, we as the audience are preparing for the final battle. And like **Saving Private Ryan**, anticipation is the predominant feeling. There can be no surprise. Not until the bell rings anyway.

This may seem more complicated than it is. All these examples demonstrate that the "preparation for the final battle" is story-dependent. There is no one right way to "prepare" for the final battle. Everything that has occurred prior to this point, along with the choice of the final battle, should lead the writer to the correct choice as to "preparation." And once more, it is the writer's job to do so, whether he uses the main character, the villain, or anyone else for that matter.

Remember what Aristotle said about unity of action: if you remove one part of the story, the remainder will be affected. The screenplay is organic in that sense. Thus, preparation is connected to what precedes it, as well as to what follows it. There is no better example of this than:

(4) *Casablanca*

The widely accepted second-act plot point in **Casablanca** occurs when Ilsa, upstairs in Rick's private quarters, tells Rick that she doesn't know what to do anymore and that he'll have to do the thinking for both of them. This follows her half-hearted attempt to force Rick to hand over the exit visas, using a gun that she rather quickly surrenders.

What follows next is a masterful combination of the writers using a well-defined main character to prepare everyone, the audience included, for the final battle.

First, Ilsa's husband, Victor Laszlo, is arrested in Rick's café that very same night. Following this, Rick takes charge and does the following: (1) he goes to the police station the next morning and makes a deal to let Captain Renault arrest Laszlo with the letters of transit; (2) he meets with Ferrari, the owner of The Blue Parrot, and arranges to sell him the American Café, while also guaranteeing employment for Sam and two other trusted employees; (3) he turns the tables on Renault that evening as Renault prepares to arrest Laszlo in the café; (4) he then instructs Renault to call the airport to arrange for the flight to take off without interference; and (5) he takes all three, Victor, Ilsa, and Renault, to the airport where someone is going to use the two exit visas to depart Casablanca.

It is only because Renault surreptitiously calls Major Strasser instead of the airport that Rick's preparations go awry. In fact, it is this action by Renault that actually sets up the final battle. If he never makes the call to Strasser, the final battle we see would never take place. Not at the airport anyway. And not in the same fashion.

Despite all the brilliant planning done by Rick, those "preparations" alone could not bring about the outcome that we eventually witness. Indeed, Rick does not foresee a "final battle" in his plan. Oh, he knows he will be arrested after the plane takes off, and he appears ready to face that event. Right up until Strasser arrives and tries to stop the plane.

The point of all this is that even the best preparations of the main character still require action or interference, if you will, from someone else. And that action or interference must be orchestrated by you, the writer, as mentioned earlier, using other characters or occurrences outside the control of the main character.

(5) *Gladiator*

As we discussed earlier, as a result of the meeting with Lucilla and Gracchus (the second-act plot point) Maximus has a plan. Thus, he does prepare for a final battle. Somewhat. He is going to escape and lead his former army into Rome. Except that before he can do either, he is thwarted in that effort in what turns out to be the "all is lost" moment. A perfect example of plans going awry.

We also discussed how the writers did this so as to get directly to the one-on-one confrontation between Maximus and Commodus. Which means that the writers had to do still more to "prepare" for the final battle. So how did they do that?

Again, as in *Witness*, the villain makes all the preparations. He schedules the battle with Maximus. He also threatens Lucilla and her son, his nephew, to insure that she will not act against his interests. And, of course, he hobbles Maximus right before they are to step out into the arena to do battle.

Like *Rocky*, nearly all the preparation Maximus performs is prior to the second-act plot point. But, as we discussed in the previous chapter, the writers could have chosen a different course so long as they ended up with a one-on-one battle between Maximus and Commodus. Had they chosen the escape-and-return scenario, then no doubt the preparation would have been in the hands of Maximus instead of Commodus. Totally story-dependent. And the product of a clear choice by the writers.

(6) *Cast Away*

Recall that the second-act plot point in this film is Chuck's rescue from his deteriorating raft. Recall also that there is no villain in this film. So what (and who) will Chuck's final battle involve?

To answer that, we must go back to the question raised at the end of act one. Our first-act plot point is Chuck washing ashore on the deserted island following the violent plane crash. The question we are then faced with is probably this: will Chuck ever get back to civilization?

If that's the case, then his rescue at the second-act plot point answers the question. But that's not really all of it, is it? For why does Chuck want to get back to civilization? Simple. He wants get back to be with Kelly, the woman he proposed to just prior to boarding the plane. So actually, the question at the end of the first act is more likely a two-part one: will Chuck ever get back to civilization and, if so, will Kelly be there waiting for him when he does?

Note that returning to Kelly is clearly Chuck's external desire. He stares at her picture in the locket while on the island. And we find out later that Kelly is, indeed, his motivation for building the raft and leaving the island. He even says her name twice when he waves to his rescuers on that tanker. Kelly is never far from Chuck's thoughts, at least those we are able to discern.

Thus, the final battle in **Cast Away** is not a one-on-one with a villain, but rather, Chuck facing his greatest desire, which also happens to present his greatest obstacle. Namely, Chuck must meet face-to-face with Kelly, hoping that she will still be waiting for him after five years of separation.

So how to prepare for this final battle? Once again, for the most part, the preparations are out of the hands of the main character. Following his rescue, we next see Chuck on board the FedEx private jet and learn from the legend on the screen that it is four weeks later. Then there is a celebration by FedEx for Chuck's return. This is clearly not Chuck's doing. In fact, he seems to be at the mercy of others throughout the entire affair.

Then comes the pivotal moment. A meeting with Kelly has been arranged. He is finally going to see her after all these years.

But when the door opens, Chuck finds his former dentist entering the room. And he quickly learns that this man is now Kelly's husband. He informs Chuck that she is not ready to see him. Kelly's husband leaves, and Chuck looks out the window to see Kelly outside in obvious distress. Her actions indicate that she is unable to decide whether to go in to see Chuck. Eventually, though, her husband gets her in the car.

We then see Chuck saying goodbye later that day to all his colleagues. They leave him alone in his suite where he observes the bounty and small miracles of everyday life that he missed while stranded on that island. Still no final battle, though.

The next scene shows Chuck alone on the floor of his room, next to his bed. It is the middle of the night and he is shining a flashlight on the locket containing the picture of Kelly. This is the last bit of preparation by the writer. Why is that?

Because in the next scene we see Chuck in a cab pulling up to a house that we suspect belongs to Kelly. Chuck gets out of the cab and walks to the front door. He is just about to ring the doorbell when the door opens to reveal Kelly awake and, it appears, waiting for him.

With that, our final battle is set to begin. Note that except for this cab ride, all of the preparation was the work of the writer using other characters and events outside of Chuck's control. But it is just as effective as Rick in *Casablanca*, who made nearly all of the preparations leading up to the final battle. Different story. Different main character. Different preparation.

(7) *Good Will Hunting*

The second-act plot point in this film occurs when Skyler asks Will to come with her to California and he refuses. More than that, in the argument that ensues he comes clean about his past and questions her love for him, believing that it won't last. She assures him that she loves him and is willing to try. When she asks him to declare his love for her, he refuses. In fact, she asks him to tell her that he *doesn't* love her. And he does. End of act two.

What follows is a series of scenes leading up to and preparing for the final battle. Yet Will is not active in those preparations, not intentionally anyway.

First, Will meets with Lambeau, the math professor, and they clash, with Will eventually destroying the latest math proof that he has solved. The scene ends with each knowing that Will is actually more advanced as a mathematician than Lambeau, his teacher. There is no more for Will to learn from him.

Next, we see Will at Chuck's house with his friends. They hang out and discuss, of all things, masturbation. And the only purpose of this scene appears to be to provide a vivid contrast with the one that follows.

Here, Will meets with a representative from the NSA about a possible job. When asked why he *shouldn't* work there, Will launches into a long and humorous explanation that only shows that Will is still resisting any attempt to get him to accept conventional employment commensurate with his skills. As in other instances where he is challenged, Will uses his superior intellect and biting humor to deflect from the matter at hand.

Will next meets with Sean, who asks him who his soul mate is. Will mentions some famous authors. Sean then shifts the conversation to what Will wants. There then follows a discussion about "honorable" jobs, such as bricklaying, which Will strenuously defends as a profession. Sean then asks if being a janitor is also honorable. Sean wonders why, of all possible places to work, Will chose to be a janitor at one of the finest mathematical institutions in the country where he solved math formulas and then lied about doing so. Will doesn't answer. Sean again asks what Will wants. Will still won't answer and so Sean makes him leave, telling him he will no longer put up with his "bullshit." Will's resistance is now at an all-time high. (This is the "all is lost" moment in this film.)

Next, Will calls Skyler to say goodbye before she leaves for California. Once again, she tells Will she loves him. But Will cannot reciprocate and simply says goodbye.

We next see Will at work on the construction site with Chuck, in one of the pivotal scenes in the movie (as we discussed in chapter two). Here, Chuck surprises Will by telling him that he (Will) is wasting his time working construction and should do more with his life. He tells Will that if he doesn't owe it to himself, he owes it to Chuck.

Finally, Lambeau and Sean argue over Will not having shown up at their last scheduled meeting. Lambeau wants Sean to force Will to take a job. Sean refuses. Their argument then turns personal, with accusations of jealousy and arrogance flying back and forth. The scene ends with Will arriving in the office for a session with Sean. It is this session that is to become the final battle.

Observe that all of this preparation involves the three important aspects of Will's life: (1) his genius/professional potential, (2) his past abuse, and (3) his inability to give and receive love. Remember that we said that preparation for the final battle is story-dependent. In **Good Will Hunting**, subplots play a big part in the overall story and, thus, make up a good portion of the preparation for the final battle. Moreover, each of the many subplots intersects with the main plot in these scenes. Note that subplots rarely intersect with the main plot and/or resolve themselves in the final battle itself. Instead, they most often cross paths with the main plot before the final battle and, if not resolved prior to that time, then they must be wrapped up in some fashion after the outcome of the final battle and just prior to the end of the film.

We will discuss more about subplots in chapter 7. For now, though, let's move on to...

Chapter Five

The Final Battle

S ounds ominous, doesn't it?

Yet every three-act story/screenplay has one. Even romantic comedies.

Perhaps "battle" isn't the right word then. It can't be if this element is to apply to comedies as well as action movies, right?

It sure can!

"Battle" implies conflict. Conflict is what it's all about. Conflict is why we watch movies. So, naturally, our main character must face some conflict. Conflict greater than he or she has ever faced before. Conflict that rises to the level of, well, a "battle."

When I first introduced the structure of the third act, I talked about choosing the last obstacle for your main character to overcome. How you might do so. And what would make the most sense both logically and from a cinematic standpoint.

But the obstacle itself is merely the event that will bring about the one-on-one confrontation we look forward to in the third act. How and where that takes place, the specifics surrounding that event, and, most of all, the choreography of what occurs make up the actual "battle."

Let's look at some of the films we have already talked about and examine the writers' choice for and execution of the "final battle."

(1) *Rocky*

Again, the final battle is obviously the fifteen-round fight between Apollo Creed and our hero, Rocky Balboa. We have known about it from the first act. We know where and when it will take place. No surprises here. Its arrival is inevitable. So what variables did Sylvester Stallone, the writer, have to consider?

Quite simply, he had to determine how the fight would progress. Which encompasses any number of choices. Remember, Rocky's stated desire is to last the full fifteen rounds. Okay. That means that at the end of the fight we will have a simple yes or no. Either he lasts or he doesn't. But is that all there is to it?

Hardly. The writer had a lot more work to do than that. He had to stage the final battle so that it gave us the maximum dramatic and emotional impact. Plus, he had to answer the questions we all have in our head when the bell rings. If Rocky is going to last, *how* will he do so? Will he employ the rope-a-dope made famous by Muhammad Ali? Run around the ring like Curly from the Three Stooges?

We know that won't happen. We've already seen Rocky fight. Stallone has already shown us. No tricks or surprises here. We know what he will do. He will lead with his head. And his heart. And so, Stallone has Rocky go right after Creed from the opening bell. And what happens?

He surprises Creed. And us. He knocks him down! That's never happened! The champ has never been knocked down! This "club" fighter from Palookaville knocks down the undisputed heavyweight champion of the world! Hey, this is going to be easier than we thought! Except, of course, it isn't. Creed's trainer sees to that. So what happens after this early "victory"?

Rocky gets pummeled pretty badly. He's on the ropes several times. He even gets knocked down himself a couple of times. Hey, this is a real slugfest! If they're not careful, somebody is going to get hurt!

And somebody does. Creed. Rocky delivers a vicious blow to Creed's ribs in the fourteenth round, and we hear the crack. We've heard that "crack" before. Back at the meat-packing plant. Just as Rocky broke the ribs on that side of beef in front of his pal Paulie, he now breaks the ribs of the heavyweight champion. In front of the whole world!

Fortunately for Creed, the bell rings, saving him from a certain defeat. So what's going to happen now? The battle is nearly over and we now find ourselves thinking: can Rocky actually win this thing?

Think of all the ways the writer could have gone with this fight. And notice how it is arranged so that entering the final round the question turns around so that we wonder now whether *Apollo* can last the entire fifteen rounds. That's good writing.

So how does it end? Does the writer dare allow Rocky to win? Sorry. We'll have to wait to discuss the outcome of this "final battle" in the next chapter.

(2) *Saving Private Ryan*

The final battle here is quite literally a battle, the battle to hold the bridge. We already know that Captain John Miller (Tom Hanks) and the rest of the ragtag outfit will be outnumbered. We already know that they will face superior firepower. We already know that it looks bleak. So what variables did the writer face in staging this battle?

Like Stallone with **Rocky**, Robert Rodat had to choreograph things. He had to show the individual skirmishes. But this battle isn't a matter of lasting fifteen rounds. This is life or death. All for a bridge.

But isn't that a secondary question? Whether or not they can hold the bridge? Remember the question that's raised at the end of the first act: can Captain Miller save Private Ryan?

While the deaths of the other Americans are tragic (though not unexpected), there is one death we do not want to contemplate. There is one soldier who must survive.

And so, for maximum dramatic impact, Robert Rodat chooses to have the American forces dwindle. He has nearly all of them die in the struggle to hold the bridge, while those few who remain alive are forced to retreat. And in so doing, he arranges the battle so that it comes down to five people: the cowardly Corporal Upham (Jeremy Davies), Private Reiben (Ed Burns), Sergeant Mike Horvath (Tom Sizemore), Captain Miller, and Private James Ryan (Matt Damon).

What happens to each? Upham (the cowardly one) is unable to act to save the life of Private Mellish, the Jewish soldier played by Adam Goldberg. Instead, Upham runs and finds a place to hide from the battle. He will be of no use in saving Ryan.

Reiben (Ed Burns) remains alive and does not hide. He fights. When I watched this film for the first time, I thought Rodat might force Reiben to make a choice between his own personal safety and protecting Ryan. I thought this would make for some pretty high drama because Burns's character expresses the most resistance to risking the squad's collective lives for Ryan.

Didn't happen. Probably because it is Captain Miller's movie and he should not be overshadowed by the heroic actions of the character whose view opposes his. Instead, Reiben somehow manages to stay alive and moves with the others to the other side of the bridge, though he eventually is separated from them.

What about Mike Horvath, the platoon sergeant? He is larger than life and a soldier in every sense of the word. He has always had the Captain's back. He does in this battle as well. In fact, he gets shot and dies while providing cover for Miller and Ryan to escape to the other side of the bridge, further decreasing the odds of Ryan being saved.

Which leaves Miller essentially alone in bearing the responsibility of saving Private Ryan. And isn't that the way it should be? The Germans have reached the opposite side of the bridge. A tank is moving slowly toward them, about to cross the short span. Miller struggles to attach the wires to the dynamite charge so that he can blow up the bridge. If he does, he can probably save both himself and Ryan. But what happens?

Miller gets blown up! Except he's not dead. He sits up. Still in one piece. Still able to save Ryan. Only now he gets shot!

But he's still not dead. So what does he do now? He moves out into the open so that he can try to fire a bullet into the explosives so that he can blow up the bridge. And save Ryan. And then—

You got it—we'll examine the outcome in the next chapter.

(3) *Witness*

Remember we said that the final battle in **Witness** is brought to John Book. He doesn't go after it. Schaeffer and the other two corrupt cops come to Lancaster County to get Book.

Okay. We know where the final battle will take place. But after that choice, the writers had the difficult task of deciding *how* that battle would take place. It would not be a fifteen-round fight. Book would not be defending a bridge. He is in the middle of Amish country, surrounded by the peaceful Amish people, and without a gun other than his own anywhere in sight.

But he also happens to be on a farm. And it's a farm that he has come to know pretty well in the two or three weeks that he has been convalescing there. While Schaeffer and the others have him outnumbered, and with more guns (as it has to be), Book has one small advantage: he is on his adopted "home" court.

Think how different the final battle would be if Book had driven back to Philadelphia and confronted Schaeffer somewhere in that metropolitan region. That would be the first problem facing the writers. Where? How does Book get them all in one place? He would need to capture or kill all three in one battle to get the job done. And he would have no reinforcements. No one he could turn to for help. Not right away. And if he had to go round them up, we would have another second act on our hands (a series of obstacles).

It makes perfect logical and cinematic sense to stage the final battle on the farm in the middle of Amish country. After all, it's what the whole movie is about. The clash of cultures. The different ways of life. And Book, while coming from the same way of life as Schaeffer, has also come to experience the Amish way.

Again, the goal of the battle is to get our main character face-to-face with the big villain. In **Rocky**, it's no problem. There is no other "villain" besides Creed. And in **Saving Private Ryan**, there is no single German villain, though the prisoner they released earlier serves as the singular representation of the enemy (remember, he's the one who shoots Miller at the end).

So how do the writers of **Witness** accomplish this? How do they get Book face-to-face with Schaeffer? In classic fashion. One at a time. In ascending order of villainy.

Recall that Book's gun is in the kitchen cupboard and he is in the barn when the bad guys arrive. He is unarmed. So he will have to use what is at his disposal in order to defend himself (and protect young Samuel).

And he does. Book kills Fergie in the silo by smothering him with corn. Lots of corn. (Note: in an earlier version of this script, it is a kicking mule that brings about Fergie's demise. Both Peter Weir and Harrison Ford found this to be rather incredible and difficult to film, leading to the change.)

Book then crawls into the bottom of the silo where he retrieves Fergie's shotgun just in time to crawl back out and fire a round into McFee before he can take proper aim and shoot Book.

Now McFee is pretty bad as villains go. He's the one who kills the undercover cop, Zenovitch, in the men's room to get the cinematic ball rolling (the killing witnessed by young Sam). He's also the one who shoots Book in his parking garage, leaving Book near death when he arrives in Amish Country. And he is one of the ones who kills Carter, Book's partner, just prior to the second-act plot point (which we see in the script, though not in the film).

But McFee is not *the* villain. Schaeffer is. He's the biggest villain of the three, because he is the power behind the corruption *and* Book's supervisor. And when they finally meet face-to-face, Book still finds himself at a disadvantage, even though Book now has Fergie's shotgun. That's because Schaeffer has his handgun pointed at the back of Rachel's head as Schaeffer enters the barn looking for Book. Again, notice how the writers choreograph the battle to wring the maximum amount of drama out of the encounter by building not only to the one-on-one, but also by giving the upper hand to the villain.

So what happens now? How does it battle turn out? You got it...

(4) *Gladiator*

You'll recall that the final battle in this film is a one-on-one fight between the villain, Commodus, and our hero, Maximus. Had to happen. Who else would Maximus do battle with? And you'll recall also that Commodus cheated just prior to the fight by stabbing Maximus in the back to help even the odds.

Unlike **Saving Private Ryan**, there isn't a lot of choreography to this battle. After all, it's a sword fight. And unlike the fight in **Rocky**, there are no rules here. No rounds. No mandatory eight counts. And unlike **Witness**, there is only one villain for our hero to face. So the writers were left with the task of deciding how long to make the battle last, keeping in mind that Maximus is fighting while he's also bleeding to death.

Commodus starts out with the upper hand. He fights well, as he should, because Maximus is dying. He even manages to slice Maximus's leg early in the fight. But in short order, Maximus turns the tide. He slices Commodus's arm and knocks away his sword.

As Maximus tries to stay upright, Commodus asks Quintus for another sword. He is refused. Now we are left to wonder, what can Commodus do? Even dying, Maximus seems to have the advantage here.

But if we've learned one thing about Commodus, it is that he always has something up his sleeve. In this case, literally. For he pulls out a long knife and attacks the staggering (and now hallucinating) Maximus.

Again, the battle here is played out so that the villain appears at least to be in a superior position to the main character. Even more so in this film, because we know right from the start of the battle that Maximus is unlikely to survive.

We'll look at how long he does so in the next chapter.

So far we've looked at films in which the final battle has closely resembled the literal meaning of the word. Let's examine two in which the "battle" is not quite so literal, but quite real nonetheless.

(1) *Cast Away*

Let's recap. The question at the end of the first act appears to be simple: will Chuck ever get off the island?

But remember, there is more to it than that. Chuck's desire is to get off the island and *return to Kelly*. Recall that when he boarded the FedEx plane in Memphis in act one, he told her he would be back soon. Oh, and they just happened to have gotten engaged moments before in the car. Chuck has her gift—the pocket watch with her picture inside—that he saved before the crash and that inspires him to stay alive on the island for those five years. That's why, in chapter 4, we amended this question to make it a two-part one: will Chuck ever get off the island and, if so, will Kelly be there for him when he does?

At the end of the second act, Chuck is rescued. So the question that immediately enters our mind now is: what happened to Kelly? Is she still waiting for Chuck? What will happen when they see one another?

When I first saw **Cast Away** and the legend on the screen informed us that it was "Four Weeks Later" when the just-rescued Chuck was flying back to Memphis in the FedEx private jet, I was rather disappointed. Hey, I thought, those were four pretty important weeks! Some significant stuff must have happened in those weeks! I felt cheated for not having seen it.

But, once again, the writer made a good choice. No doubt some important stuff happened off-screen in those four weeks. But those things were not crucial to the main story. For the question that most requires answering is: will Chuck get back to Kelly?

And if that doesn't get answered in those four weeks, then they don't much matter, do they?

So where's the "battle," you ask? If not in Chuck's adjustment just after his rescue, then where? Well, remember our discussion in the previous chapter.

Following the aborted meeting that was arranged for Chuck and Kelly at the FedEx "welcome home" party, we eventually see Chuck pull up in a cab outside Kelly's house. And when Kelly opens the door and lets him in we have the beginning of our final battle.

But wait, you say, they don't argue. They don't fight. They don't even raise their voices. How can that be a battle?

Here's where we have the debate about the use of that word. It is not a "battle" in the traditional sense, but what Chuck and Kelly say to one another and what happens as a result of their meeting will most certainly decide Chuck's fate with respect to Kelly. Just like the battle in the barn decides John Book's fate with respect to protecting little Samuel from Schaeffer. Just like the battle on the bridge decides Captain Miller's fate with respect to saving Private Ryan. And just like the fifteen-round fight decides Rocky's fate with respect to proving to everyone that he is not a tomato.

The point is that the final battle does not have to lead to bloodshed or fisticuffs. It simply has to decide the main character's cinematic fate. It has to answer the question raised at the end of the first act. Just like those where blood is involved, these "battles" must be one-on-one, face-to-face. And the main character's life has to be in the balance, if not literally, then figuratively.

We'll come back to the outcome of this battle in the next chapter. But for now, let's examine:

(2) *Good Will Hunting*

This film is told in three acts, though I am sure that some enterprising soul could break it down into five or seven. But for the sake of our examination, let's stick to three.

Doing so, we said our second-act plot point occurs when Skyler asks Will to tell her he doesn't love her. And he does. So what is the final obstacle facing our hero? What can be greater than those he's faced already in his troubled life?

How about everything all rolled into one? His genius. His past. His friends. His future. The math professor. Skyler. Everything.

Where does all that reside? Where is all that conflict?

Why, it's all inside Will, isn't it? It's been bottled up in there for years. So how the heck does one have a battle with all that? It's internal, isn't it? Isn't "internal" taboo in film?

No doubt. Except when there is some external force or circumstance against which it can play out. For instance, in **Casablanca**, Rick's conflict is also internal, but it plays out *externally* through the exit visas and Ilsa and Laszlo and Captain Renault and Major Strasser.

In **Good Will Hunting**, there is only one person and place where such a "battle" can take place. That's right, through Sean in Sean's office.

Look at what the writers did earlier in this script. They put Will's life in jeopardy by having him face incarceration. And to avoid that, he is forced by the legal system to see a therapist to deal with his violent tendencies. And to deal with his genius, he is also ordered by the court to meet with the math professor who has "discovered" his genius.

Notice that those things are interrelated. Will won't use his genius because to do so, he fears, will force him to become separated from his friends who are the only "family" he has ever been able to rely upon. And the reason for that is because he was abused as a child in his foster homes and didn't receive the love a normal child might have expected. Which is why he doesn't trust anyone (like Skyler) who says they love him. Oh, and also why he has some rather violent tendencies.

Who else could sort out all of this but a therapist? Because it is in therapy that we examine our past and try to understand its influence on our current behavior. Sean, as a skilled therapist, represents the greatest opposing force in Will's life.

Look at it another way: what other choice did the writers have? The final battle couldn't be a literal battle, a fight. That wouldn't address the complexity of Will's emotional and psychological problems. And the final battle surely couldn't be a math problem or an argument with the math professor. That would have been an appallingly bad screenwriting choice.

The only other possible character through whom Will could play out his emotional drama is Skyler. And he does, sort of. But this not being a romantic comedy, the final battle could not be with his love interest. In this case, she has to be the goal, not the method through which he achieves it.

So if a meeting with Sean is the obvious choice for the final battle, then how could the writers show an outcome? We'll find out the answer to that in the next chapter.

So what to learn from these last two examples?

The final battle does not always have to involve guns or fists or bloodshed. It merely has to be a confrontation. Usually one with another person, though that other person does not always have to be the villain. They can simply be a physical being with whom the main character struggles to resolve their dilemma. Which is just another way of saying that the "battle" with this person is simply the device the writer employs to answer the question raised at the end of the first act.

That said, we now turn to...

Chapter Six

The Outcome of the Final Battle

Answers.

In a word, that's what the reader/audience is looking for at the end of the final battle. Whatever the outcome, they want answers.

More specifically, they want to know the answer to the question you, the screenwriter, raised at the end of the first act. That is the whole point of the third act. And the final battle within it.

Remember: *you* prepare for that battle. *You* orchestrate where and how it will take place. And with whom. It is also up to you to decide its outcome.

Most screenwriting instructors tell their students that they must know their ending before they begin writing their script. I agree. Except with the choice of words. I have a somewhat different theory on what constitutes the "ending" of a movie, which you will hear about in chapter 9.

For now, though, let me give you my version of that statement about knowing your ending. In my view, you don't need to know your "ending" before you start to write. But you must know "the outcome of the final battle" before you begin to put fingers to keyboard.

Now, notice what I didn't say. I didn't say that you need to know what the final battle is precisely. Or how it is set up. You needn't know where and how it takes place. Or its choreography. But you do need to know generally what the outcome will be of any final battle involving your main character.

Why?

Because again, that outcome will answer the question you raised at the end of the first act. And you must know the answer to the question you formulate before you create the obstacles in the path of your main character. And you must know the answer to that question before you bring us into the third act.

Are there exceptions to this? Absolutely. Writers often change the outcome of their final battle when they rewrite their scripts. Happens all the time. But that only means that the writer "knew" the outcome when they wrote their first draft. And for some good reason, in the process of rewriting they discovered something else about their story and/or their main character that caused them to change the outcome.

Why would they do that?

Quite simply, to best serve the story. It has been said of screen-writing that it is all about choices. It has also been said that you find out which choices work by finding out which choices *don't* work. Hey, we're all wrong from time to time. Even about our scripts.

Nevertheless, you must "know" the outcome of the final battle before you start to write. Thereafter, if that outcome does not suit the story as well as another outcome, you are free to change it. Indeed, you must change it, because the outcome of the final battle is crucial to the reader's evaluation of your script.

This is true because that outcome answers the question you caused the reader/audience to ponder for the entire second act, and right into the third. It is what the movie is all about. Remember? Question and answer.

You'll recall that I pointed out some examples of films where the question raised at the end of the first act was not the same as the main character's stated desire. And I said that you must provide an answer to that desire. However, you do not necessarily have to provide that answer with the outcome of the final battle. There is still time to do so after the final battle has been decided. (More on this in chapter 7.)

With all that in mind, let's look at the films we have talked about to see what the outcomes of those final battles were, and how they answered the questions raised by those writers in their first acts.

(1) *Saving Private Ryan*

The question raised at the end of the first act in **Saving Private Ryan** is simple: can Captain Miller save Private Ryan? The final battle is literally that, a battle, one waged against a German army far superior in number and firepower to the small group of Americans defending that bridge. Against great odds, no?

So what is the outcome of that battle? In short, Miller saves Private Ryan. He gets him over the bridge and behind a wall, where he remains safe until the American reinforcements arrive. But in the process of saving Ryan, Miller himself dies. We have our answer. But along with that answer, we get an unexpected (maybe) consequence of Miller's efforts.

No doubt, many moviegoers were saddened by the death of Miller on that bridge. After all, nobody wants to see Tom Hanks die. But as we discussed, that was the whole point of the movie. Which was about World War II. Which was all about sacrifice.

In an earlier version of the script, Captain Miller saves Ryan and survives. Somewhere along the line, Robert Rodat changed the "outcome." Or did he?

Think about it. In both versions, Ryan is saved. In the one that was filmed and released, Miller dies in the process. Only a *part* of the outcome was changed. That part dealt with the consequence of Miller saving Ryan. But in changing that part of the outcome, the writer made a statement about war. And the value of human life. And, yes, sacrifice.

Would the film have been received differently had Miller survived as in that earlier version? No question. In my opinion, the filmed version was superior and the correct choice.

(2) *Rocky*

Every year, I am amazed at how many of my students who have only heard about the original **Rocky** but haven't yet seen it think that Rocky wins the fight. Some even think so after having seen it!

As you'll recall, the final battle is the fight itself. And the outcome is that Rocky survives the entire fifteen rounds. There is raucous celebration afterward. Almost lost amidst the uproar is the judges' decision: Rocky loses in a split decision.

Now our main character losing a prizefight would ordinarily make for a letdown at the end of a movie. It's not an outcome many screenwriters would choose. Which is probably why so many people think Rocky won.

But in this case it works. Really works. Why?

The question raised at the end of the first act is probably open to interpretation. But I think the fairest choice would be: what's going to happen to this club fighter when he gets into the ring with the heavyweight champion of the world? Does any one of us dare to ask if he will win? Maybe there's a part of us that wonders. But we've seen Rocky fight. And we've heard about him from Micky and others. He's a tomato.

Besides, the second question (will he win?) gets pretty much answered for us when we learn of Rocky's revised desire. More specifically, you'll recall that in the beginning of the third act Rocky tells Adrian that he can't win, but only wants to go the distance. The Rock goes from wanting to prove himself in a general sense in the second act, to wanting only to survive the full fifteen rounds at the beginning of the third act. In fact, he tells us that lasting the fifteen rounds will prove that he is "not just another bum from the neighborhood."

Certainly, in the first and second acts Rocky lets it be known to

Micky and others that he is not a "tomato"—that he still can be somebody. But that doesn't seem to create the question at the end of the first act.

In any case, it doesn't matter. With the outcome of the final battle, we get an answer to any question raised at the end of the first act. However you define it. He doesn't win, but he does something that no one has ever done before—he goes the distance with the champ. *That's* what happens to him when he gets in the ring. And in doing so, he proves he's not a tomato and is "somebody."

Notice also that it answers the main character's stated desire as well. Rocky lasts the full fifteen rounds. All of the questions are covered in this "outcome of the final battle."

As with **Saving Private Ryan**, ponder how would you feel about this movie if, as some of my students think, Rocky were to actually defeat the champ? Would it be realistic, given all we have heard about both Apollo and Rocky prior to the fight? Would it change your thinking about the film? We'll save that discussion for a later chapter.

(3) *Gladiator*

As in **Rocky**, the final battle here is a one-on-one fight. Only this one has much higher stakes. It will end only when one of the combatants is dead.

When we left off in chapter 5, Maximus was dying and Commodus was about to attack him with the knife he pulled out of his sleeve. But Maximus comes out of his reverie and gets back in the fight. He beats Commodus with his fists. Then he turns the knife around on Commodus and sticks it in his throat, killing the evil emperor.

We have the outcome of the final battle. Maximus defeats Commodus. But does that answer the question raised at the end of the first act?

Recall that we had some debate about that question. One could say it was: will Maximus fulfill Marcus Aurelius's request to

transform Rome back into a republic? Except that we thought
Maximus's enslavement and new-found career as a gladiator put
that question out of our minds.

One could also argue that the question is: will Maximus get
revenge on Commodus for killing his family? And if that is the
question, we most certainly have our answer.

But what happens immediately following the death of Commodus answers that first question as well. For, as Maximus stag-
gers about, "seeing" the door to his home, he is called back to
consciousness by Quintus. Coming around, Maximus orders that
his men be freed and that Gracchus be reinstated as senator and
that Rome be made a republic, as requested by Marcus Aurelius
just prior to his death.

Maximus then collapses and dies. As in **Saving Private Ryan**,
the outcome of the final battle has a consequence: the main character dies. Nevertheless, we have an answer to whatever question
you might have in mind at the end of the first act.

But that's not all. We'll discuss the rest of what happens in
Gladiator in chapter 7.

(4) *Witness*

The final battle in this film takes place in the barn on the Amish
farm. And when we discussed it in the previous chapter, Book had
eliminated two of the villains and was now facing off against
Schaeffer, his main nemesis, with Schaeffer holding a gun to the
head of the Amish woman Rachel Lapp. In the ensuing standoff,
Book gives up the shotgun and Schaeffer, keeping the gun to
Rachel's head, leads them outside where young Samuel has
already rung the bell, which is the Amish cry for help.

So what's the outcome? Does Book somehow wrestle the gun
from Schaeffer and kill him? Does Eli find Book's gun in the
kitchen cupboard and shoot Schaeffer?

No. Schaeffer, Book, and Rachel emerge to find about twenty
Amish men, women, and children standing outside waiting. Watch-

ing. Schaeffer feebly declares that Book is wanted for murder and that he, Schaeffer, is there to take him in. But he convinces no one.

Instead, Book moves away from Schaeffer to stand alongside the Amish. He then asks Schaeffer what he intends to do? Shoot him? Shoot Eli? Shoot young Samuel? And it quickly becomes clear that Schaeffer is helpless. He can do nothing. Because if he does decide to kill Book or anyone else, he will not get away with it. Standing there will be twenty "witnesses" to his misdeed.

Pretty good outcome. The clear question at the end of the first act is, will John Book protect his witness (Samuel) from the corrupt Philadelphia police officers? The answer to that question is yes. It is also the answer to the main character's desire, because they are one and the same. (His earlier desire to solve the case evolved rather quickly into protecting Samuel at all costs. "There isn't going to be any trial," he tells Rachel early in the second act.)

How this outcome comes about is what makes the movie so enjoyable. Were Book to have killed Schaeffer along with the other two bad cops, it would not have served the story as well. Remember, this movie is about the differences between the two cultures. In an important scene in the second act, Eli tells Samuel about the Amish way, which is to avoid violence. "There's always another way," he tells his grandson. And the outcome of the final battle not only answers the question from the first act, but also serves to reinforce the theme of the movie.

I don't know, but I'm willing to guess that the writers knew from the beginning that Book would protect Samuel (the outcome). But I would guess also that it took some time and several rewrites before they reached the ultimate "outcome" in which Book is aided by the Amish with whom he has lived for a few weeks.

Regardless, there is an outcome that answers our question(s) and serves the theme of the entire story as well.

(5) *Cast Away*

Recall that in this film, the final battle is not a traditional "battle." No guns, no fists, no bloodshed. Instead, Chuck goes to see Kelly, his former fiancée, whom he had left at the Memphis airport five years before. He knows now that she has remarried, which will no doubt influence the outcome of this "battle."

After discussing what Kelly did in the months and years following Chuck's disappearance, Kelly returns Chuck's Jeep to him. But they still haven't discussed what he came there to talk about, namely, his love for her and hers for him, if indeed any remains.

Nevertheless, Chuck drives off, only to be chased down by Kelly in the pouring rain. Okay, we think, this is it. She's going to tell him that she loves him. That he is the love of her life. And she does! And Chuck tells her that he still loves her! And that he never should have gotten on that plane! And—

And then Chuck realizes that it simply cannot be as it was. He did get on that plane. And Kelly must now go back inside. To her husband and child. To her new life. The life that no longer has room for Chuck. And he lets her do so.

The question raised at the end of the first act is: will Chuck ever get off the island and, if so, will Kelly be waiting there for him when he does? Remember, we learn in the second act that his desire is not simply to return home, but to return to Kelly, who he had intended to marry. Might you say then that the question and desire were the same at the end of the first act? Maybe. But it doesn't matter, because the outcome answers both.

Yes, Chuck does return home. And he does return to Kelly. But, as in *Saving Private Ryan*, there is a bit of a twist. Kelly is no longer available. She is quite married. So Chuck has satisfied his desire, but not in the way he (or we) might have imagined.

Whenever I poll my class about this, I usually find that about a third of the class is disappointed in this "outcome." And we talk about why that is. I happen to fall into the two-thirds that find this outcome to be okay. Preferable, in fact, to an available Kelly and a more "happy" reunion. We'll discuss why that is in a later chapter.

(6) *Good Will Hunting*

The question at the end of act one is (arguably), what is going to happen to Will following his release from jail now that he has been ordered to meet with both a therapist and the math professor? An ancillary question might be: will he continue to work as a janitor at MIT or move on to something more fitting with his abilities?

We said that the final battle in this film is an internal one in which Will is forced to face his past and the long-buried feelings about his upbringing. This battle, though internal, is waged in Sean's office following Sean's revelation of his court-ordered psychological report on Will.

And the outcome?

Simple. A breakthrough. When Sean and Will begin to discuss the respective beatings they each took as youngsters, it all comes tumbling out in the famous "it's not your fault" scene. Sean repeats that phrase over and over to Will, making him break down. How? Will cries. Not something we ever expect to see from him. Crying can only mean one thing: Will is feeling something. And if he is feeling something, then that is a breakthrough.

As with **Saving Private Ryan**, William Goldman had a comment about this film as well. In particular, he questioned this "outcome." Simply put, he didn't buy it. And I understand his objection. Would the simple repetition of that phrase really lead to a psychological breakthrough for someone like Will? In the real world, probably not. But in the world of cinema, particularly Will's world, in which we suspect he has never had a conversation with anyone about his "feelings" on any level, we can probably swallow it. Having considered all of the other options for a final battle in chapter 5, I think it is as good a choice as any the writers could have come up with.

Still, we must ask whether this "outcome" answers the question raised in the first act?

If the question is, what will happen to Will after being forced to meet with the math professor and a therapist? then we have our answer: Will has a breakthrough.

But what about the whole janitor thing? Nope. Not answered.

What about Skyler? Will he get together with Skyler? Not answered either.

And what about his stated desire to remain in South Boston with Chuck and the others for the rest of his life? Likewise, not answered.

But as with the previous two questions, we have a pretty darn good idea what the answer to that one might be.

Following Will's breakthrough in Sean's office, do we really think that Will is going to go back to being a janitor at MIT or anywhere else?

Do we think he will abandon all thought of Skyler and simply move on to the next girl only to break it off with her as soon as he starts to feel something? If so, then those tears were false. No, we don't think that will happen at all.

And what about South Boston and Chuck? We already have our answer. We just haven't seen it yet.

Yes, the outcome of the final battle in **Good Will Hunting** answers the question(s) we have at the end of the first act. And it makes everything else that happens thereafter seem inevitable. And that is very good.

In conclusion, the outcome of the final battle must answer the question you raised at the end of your first act, though not necessarily the main character's stated desire, should that be a separate question. And you should know this outcome before you start to write. Or should you? Remember, you should "know" the outcome, but should your story evolve over time and rewrites such that the "outcome" you envisioned when you began to write no longer serves the story or your theme, you should select a different outcome. Or, perhaps, consider an unexpected consequence of that outcome for your main character.

So what then? Once you've done that, once you have answered the question raised at the end of the first act and considered all possible consequences, is your work done? Is it time to write "FADE OUT" and send the reader/audience on their way?

For the answer to that question, let's look at the fourth element of the structure of the third act...

Chapter Seven

The Denouement

Imagine the feeling you would have had if **Saving Private Ryan** had "ended" and the credits rolled immediately after Captain Miller's hand stopped shaking, indicating that he had drawn his last breath. Bad enough that Tom Hanks has died on screen. But now we're expected to walk outside and get in our cars and head home?

Or try to picture your reaction if, after Will breaks down in tears in Sean's office in **Good Will Hunting**, the screen went to black and credits rolled. Would you have the same feelings about that film?

Despite the obvious implication, movies don't end with the "outcome of the final battle." Sure, the outcome answers the question(s) raised by the writer at the end of the first act. In that sense, there is a conclusion. But we crave more as moviegoers, don't we? We're not ready just yet to let go of the story or its characters, are we?

Which is why every great ending needs a "denouement."

The Webster's Dictionary definition of "denouement" is: "(t)he final disentangling of the intricacies of a plot, as of a drama or novel." And, technically, that is accurate with respect to movies as well. But it is far more than that.

In the context of our third act structure, we might simply define the term "denouement" as "all of the scenes that follow the outcome of the final battle."

An even simpler definition might be that the denouement is the main character's reaction to the outcome of the final battle. I think that is both accurate and a good guidepost for helping the writer decide what scene or scenes should be included in the denouement. However, I think that definition is a bit limiting.

The denouement can and should involve more than just the main character. For instance, when the main character dies in the outcome of the final battle, there is not likely to be much response on his or her part. So we can add to that definition by saying that the denouement is the main character's and/or the rest of the world's reaction to the outcome of the final battle.

In addition, in movies, the denouement can also serve other, quite specific purposes, the number of which may depend on the story. It is all based upon what best suits the script and the story the writer wants to tell. Let's take a look at some of those purposes.

Cooling-Off Period

The denouement often serves as a "cooling-off period." In this instance, the denouement is the time after the outcome of the final battle when we gather our thoughts and begin to grasp the meaning of what we have just seen. Certainly, this is true in a film such as *Saving Private Ryan*.

Resolving Subplots

The denouement often serves as the time and place in the story for resolving those subplots that have not yet been wrapped up prior to the outcome of the final battle. As a writer, you must resolve all your subplots. To not do so will leave the audience feeling that there are "loose ends," which is the moviegoer's term for unresolved subplots. The denouement is the part of the script best suited for doing that, more often than not.

A Curtain Call

In comedies in particular, the denouement often acts as a sort of "curtain call" for the characters we have come to know and love over the previous ninety to one hundred minutes. Just like in the theater, the characters are brought out one more time for us to see them, applaud their performance, and appreciate everything that has just taken place.

A Final Farewell

Somewhat related to the curtain call, the denouement may act as a final farewell. Instead of the characters saying goodbye to us, it can be an opportunity for *us* to say goodbye to some of them so that they can go back into their world. Put another way, this is us seeing them off safely, just as you would with your kids at the bus stop each morning.

Answer the Main Character's Stated Desire

Finally, if the question that is raised at the end of the first act is different from the main character's stated desire, the denouement may be where the writer will provide an "answer" to the question of whether our main character achieves their expressed desire.

Simply put, every third act must have a denouement. There is no exception to this, in my opinion. It is required. Otherwise, we end up with a feeling such as the ones we might have experienced if those films mentioned above had ended with just the outcome of the final battle.

Which can mean the waste of some valuable writing. For no matter how well thought out the setup of the final battle, the final battle itself, and the outcome of the final battle may be, you the writer cannot create a great ending without a denouement. Indeed, you the writer cannot create a great ending without a *great* denouement.

Having said that, the denouement does not have to be very long, nor should it be. Some "great" films, in fact, have quite short denouements. This is okay, so long as they have one. ***Thelma & Louise*** appears not to have one at all, for instance. The women simply go over the cliff in the convertible in the final shot of the film. It is stunning, but oddly satisfying as well. There are no scenes after this one, which is obviously the outcome of the final battle. But note that director Ridley Scott does not send the audience out of the theater on that note. Instead, as the credits begin to roll, he shows us scenes from earlier in the film (without the dialogue). And they are not just any scenes. They are scenes where the two women are happy. A curtain call, if you will, before we say goodbye.

Remember those screenwriting experts who say that you must know your "ending" before you begin to write? We talked about how they were actually referring to knowing the "outcome of the final battle," which actually means knowing the answer to the question you raise at the end of the first act.

Well, this bit of instruction does not mean that you must know your denouement prior to beginning the writing process. In fact, in the vast majority of scripts, you will not decide upon your denouement, either in part or in its entirety, until after several drafts of the script have been written.

Why is that?

Look back at the purposes of the denouement and you will have your answer. If one of the purposes of your denouement is to resolve subplots, it is unlikely that, prior to writing the script, you will have completely developed your subplots to a point where you will know not only where they intersect with the main plot, but also where they naturally find their resolution in your story.

Likewise, if your main character's stated desire is not the same as the question you raised at the end of the first act, that decision by you is likely to have come about after several rewrites, since this involves the intricacies of the plot. And intricacies of plot develop over multiple rewrites.

Certainly, if you are writing a comedy, you can plan on a curtain call ahead of time. But you probably cannot predict the specific setting in which that curtain call will take place. This is true because in the writing process you may come up with an earlier event that you wish to revisit at the absolute end to show a change in the circumstances of the main character. And it is asking a great deal of the screenwriter to outline so thoroughly that such a connective thread is envisioned before ever turning on the computer.

One final note: your denouement does not have to satisfy all of those purposes listed above. Satisfying this element of the structure of the third act may only require one scene. Or it may demand a series of scenes, each of which satisfies a different purpose. It totally depends on your story. But regardless of the story you have chosen, you want to be careful not to go on too long after the outcome of the final battle or you will lose the impact of that outcome.

Having said all that, let's look at some of the films we've talked about so far to see what the writers did with the denouement.

(1) *Good Will Hunting*

This movie is great because it has multiple subplots that are woven beautifully into the main plot, and all of which connect certain parts of the movie with other parts. Audiences love it when there are connective threads running through a film. That's because we love it when what occurs on screen happens because of something that preceded it. In other words, we love it when events seem to happen "naturally" and are not episodic in nature.

In **Good Will Hunting**, following Will's breakthrough, there are a number of subplots left to be resolved. Also, while Will's breakthrough answers the question raised at the end of the first act, it does not answer the question raised by Will's stated desire. We know what has happened to Will following the judge's

requirement that he see a therapist (the breakthrough), but we
don't know if he will stay in South Boston for the rest of his life.
As stated in the previous chapter, we know there can be only one
answer to this question, but we still want to see it.

Following the outcome of the final battle in this film, the following subplots are resolved: (1) Will is going to take a job as
something more than a janitor (just not the one he tells Sean
about); (2) Sean is going to get back in the game and travel the
world, inspired by his relationship and conversations with Will;
(3) Will is going to leave his beloved South Boston buds; (4)
Chuck is going to have his fondest wish fulfilled (Will makes
something of himself); (5) Sean and Lambeau (the math professor) resolve their differences and agree to meet at the next MIT
reunion; and (6) Will takes off for California to find Skyler and
give himself a chance to find out what it feels like to love someone
and, perhaps, even make a family of his own. Whew.

Note that numbers (3) and (6) together also answer the question regarding Will's stated desire to stay in South Boston for the
rest of his life.

With any one of these subplots left unresolved, this film would
be nowhere near as "great" or as fulfilling as it is.

(2) *Rocky*

Recall that the outcome of the final battle (Rocky lasts the full fifteen rounds) answers both the question raised at the end of the
first act (what will happen when Rocky steps into the ring with
Apollo Creed?) as well as Rocky's stated desire (to go the full fifteen rounds). So what's left?

Rocky doesn't have as many subplots as **Good Will Hunting**.
But it still has quite a few. Rocky's previous occupation as a leg-
breaker is a subplot, and it is resolved when Rocky lasts in the ring
with Creed. We know now that he won't have to go back to his
gangster friend Gazzo for work. Micky, as Rocky's trainer, is
resolved in the final battle (in the ring) as well. With Rocky's performance in the fight, we know they are firmly reunited.

How about Adrian and the love-interest subplot? Well, in that famous post-fight scene, when Rocky screams her name and they express their love for one another, that subplot is certainly resolved. After all we've gone through with this couple, this is one subplot that cannot be left unresolved. Indeed, we come to realize that the one person Rocky wants to prove himself to is Adrian, maybe even more so than to himself. Because of this, I often think *Rocky* is really a love story with a boxing subplot.

But what about the subplot involving Adrian's brother, Paulie, and Rocky? Remember Paulie's fervent desire to capitalize on Rocky's newfound fame? This one is resolved *prior* to the fight, with the robe that Paulie convinces Rocky to wear advertising Shamrock Meats, Inc., the meat-packing plant where Paulie works. Rocky dons the robe as he walks into the ring, signifying that he has compromised and allowed his friend to earn some money off of his notoriety.

The last subplot involves the strained relationship between Paulie and his sister, Adrian, and it is resolved in the denouement. In the pandemonium after the fight, Adrian tries to enter the ring but is prevented from doing so by a cop. She looks at her brother pleadingly and just says his name. Nothing more. And Paulie lifts the rope to allow her to sneak into the ring. One simple action, and the entire subplot is masterfully resolved. In doing what he does, Paulie gives Adrian his "permission" to leave him and go with Rocky. This subplot requires resolution, and to do so *after* the fight is a nice touch. And to do so with action and not dialogue is pretty darn good writing.

The denouement in *Rocky* is short, resolves all the remaining unresolved subplots, and provides us with an opportunity to say goodbye to Rocky and Adrian, knowing that they will be more than all right after this event in their lives. Cynics out there might say that it also provides a pretty nice setup for the sequels to follow, but I doubt very much that any of the filmmakers could have foreseen the phenomenal success of this picture at the time the denouement was shot and edited.

(3) *Cast Away*

After Chuck leaves Kelly's house knowing that they cannot be together again, we see him talking with his coworker about what happened both at Kelly's house that night and on the island for those five long years. (More about this in chapter 8.)

The next time we see Chuck, the sun is shining and he is driving in his Jeep to deliver the FedEx package he kept with him for the entire time on the island. We see also that the woman to whom he must deliver it is not at home. So Chuck leaves a note for her at her ranch and drives away.

He then finds himself at a crossroad, both literally and figuratively, looking at a map when the woman whose package it is pulls over. Except he doesn't know it's her. She tells him where he is and offers him some choices as to which direction he might take. Then she hops back into her truck and drives off.

As she does, Chuck sees the winged symbol on the tailgate and realizes it matches the one on the package and at the ranch. Our last shot is Chuck looking down the road the woman is driving on back to the ranch. While we don't know for certain, we are clearly left with the impression that Chuck will opt to go in that direction.

Subplots?

There are relatively few in **Castaway**. The package could qualify as a subplot, in which case it is resolved as discussed above. Chuck's job is certainly a subplot. This FedEx subplot is resolved pretty much prior to the final battle, when Chuck is welcomed back and it is implied that they will do anything for him. Plus, at Kelly's, we see how famous he has become and we have no concern about how he will make a living.

Chuck's stated desire? As we learned, it is to return home to Kelly, which he does in the final battle, though it does not turn out as he had hoped.

So, apart from the package subplot, what is the purpose of this denouement?

A "cooling off"? Maybe. Although I would argue that the outcome of the final battle is not an action-packed one and, thus, does not really require time for us to settle down and reflect. But that doesn't mean that there isn't a reason for the film to go on after the outcome of the final battle has been determined.

Indeed, these scenes seem to be there to show us that Chuck will be all right after letting go of Kelly. They are designed for us to let him go, as well. And, yes, to say our goodbyes. Not really a curtain call, but a final farewell, knowing that if Chuck goes after that woman, we're pretty sure he will be okay.

We will talk more on these scenes (one in particular) in a later chapter.

(4) *Saving Private Ryan*

In the outcome of the final battle, Captain Miller "saves" Private Ryan. But he dies in the process. As we know, his stated desire is the same as the question raised at the end of the first act. Captain Miller saving Private Ryan answers both questions.

But are there any subplots left to be resolved? It seems that all of those involving the other soldiers have been resolved in the battle. In the case of those who die, their death (and sacrifice) is certainly resolution.

So how about a final farewell? Captain Miller is our main character and, unfortunately, he will not be okay after this event in his life. Whether we like it or not, we have to say goodbye to Miller on that bridge.

What about a curtain call? Well, *Saving Private Ryan* is hardly a comedy. And it is not a drama in which a curtain call would serve any good purpose.

So why do we need a denouement?

Well, there is someone else to consider, isn't there?

Remember, this movie is framed. It opens at the cemetery in Normandy in present day. Because of his age and facial similarities, the older man we see could be either Captain Miller or James

Ryan. When the movie opens, we don't know which it is. So we have to go back to him.

And we do so by having Ryan's face morph into the old man's. okay, that's answered. But we still have some questions, don't we? It would not be unfair to suggest that this modern Ryan-at-the-cemetery is a subplot. But it could also be said to be a final farewell to Ryan, though he is not our main character.

This is so because we are left wondering how Ryan feels about all of this. And the question is not only one that occurs naturally to us, but is also raised by Miller's famous (and awkward) last words on the bridge when he instructs Ryan to "earn this."

Thus, the denouement presents a scene in which Ryan asks his wife if he's been a good man, whether he has lived a "good life." And she assures him that he has done both.

I suspect this denouement was added late in the writing process. An earlier version of the script in which Miller survives has no such scene, for obvious reasons.

In addition to providing a final farewell and a resolving of the cemetery subplot, these scenes also act as a cooling-off period, because the battle scene that precedes them is stirring and requires some settling in afterward. In fact, this is a classic example of the denouement as a cooling-off period.

One could also say that these scenes are used to relieve the negative impression left by the prior scenes in which Captain Miller dies following his instruction to Ryan. Relieving a negative created by the outcome of the final battle can also be a purpose of the denouement. In the case of this film, it was a wise choice to include these scenes.

In addition, these scenes seem to have been added to reinforce the theme of this film, which is about the sacrifice of war. Reinforcing a theme can also be a purpose served by the denouement. Once again, this works particularly well in this film.

Having said all that, there is still an aspect of this denouement that did not ring true for me.

At one point, Ryan's wife reads the headstone and asks her husband who Captain Miller was. Ryan tells her just a tiny fraction of who Miller was and what he meant to Ryan.

Now, it has been widely observed over the years that many veterans of World War II did not talk about their experiences, even to their closest family members. And I have no doubt that Spielberg was trying to illustrate that point with this scene.

However, it would seem to me that James and his wife would have had some discussions about their families at some point in their forty-some years of courtship and marriage. And at some point, Ryan's brothers would had to have come up. Prospective spouses naturally inquire about brothers and sisters. And at some point, the return of James following the death of his three brothers in the same week during World War II would had to have been discussed. How else to explain his safe return?

Look at it from this standpoint: would Ryan have lied to his wife about how his return from the war came about? Or would he have downplayed it to the point of leaving her to think that it was no big thing? Would a "good man" do such a thing?

And would Ryan's mother not have known? After all, she knows her other sons died. And we learn earlier in the denouement that she received a letter announcing James's impending return (and prior bravery). Would she have been sworn to secrecy in any conversations she might have had with James's wife about James's service in the war?

The idea behind *Saving Private Ryan* is such a good one simply because it is so compelling on a basic human level. If it were a true story, would it be realistic for anyone to have kept the circumstances of their being saved in such a dramatic fashion a secret from their own family?

This may seem a small matter perhaps. But in attempting to illustrate a rather minor aspect of the war's aftermath (veterans not talking about their experiences), I believe Spielberg took away from the noble and oft-reinforced theme of sacrifice, which permeates this film.

(5) *Witness*

Like **Rocky**, this film features a relatively short denouement. In the outcome of the final battle, Schaeffer surrenders to Book. Following this, we next see Book (from Samuel and Rachel's point of view) outside with the police who have arrived to take custody of Schaeffer and sort out what has just occurred. This scene is followed by one with Book and Samuel sitting by the pond. Book whispers something we can't hear. Then they say goodbye.

The next scene is Book on the porch with Rachel standing in the doorway of the house. Okay, we think, this is it. We are going to hear them say goodbye. Only we don't. Instead, they look at one another. Finally, they exchange smiles and Book steps off the porch. Not a word is spoken. But I suspect we all know how they feel about one another just by those looks.

Interestingly, in an earlier version of the script, there were two pages of dialogue between the two. This was trimmed down to less than one. And when the film was cut and edited, the choice was to have no words spoken at all. A wise choice indeed. For anything they might say, we already know and feel.

The next scene is Book getting in his car. Eli calls out to Book to "be careful out among them English." This is what Eli said to Rachel as she boarded the train early in the first act, and it indicates that Eli now accepts Book (almost) as one of them. Those simple words masterfully resolve the subplot between the two.

The final scene before the credits roll is Book driving up the road leading out of the farm where he stops to say his goodbyes to Daniel Hochleitner (Alexander Gudunov), who we believe will become Rachel's husband sometime soon (another subplot resolved).

That may seem like a lot of scenes, but they only add up to about two minutes of screen time. In that short time, we get subplots wrapped up and a chance to say a final farewell to all the major characters. Quite an effective and efficient denouement.

(6) *Gladiator*

When we left off in the previous chapter, Commodus had died, and Maximus had ordered the reinstatement of Gracchus and the re-establishment of Rome as a republic. Then Maximus collapsed.

Now, one can argue that everything after Commodus dies is really the denouement. I wouldn't object very strongly to that. But it is somewhat academic because what follows Maximus's collapse clearly makes up all or part of the denouement.

As Maximus lay dying, Lucilla (the emperor's sister) implores him to "go to them," referring to Maximus's wife and son who he now "sees," presumably in the afterlife. He then dies, and thereafter reunites with his family. Note that this is Maximus's expressed desire in the first act. Recall that we said that once we saw them dead, we assumed he could no longer fulfill this desire. But we were wrong. The writers cleverly satisfy this want on Maximus's part by reuniting them in the afterlife.

Looking back, perhaps we shouldn't have been so quick to abandon this want on his part. After all, throughout the film, Maximus keeps the small figures representing his wife and son. He obviously doesn't abandon all thought of them. So we shouldn't be surprised then when he is finally able to be with them again.

Maximus's death is followed by Lucilla instructing those around him to "honor him." Gracchus then steps forward and asks who will carry him. Maximus is then taken from the floor of the Colosseum, presumably to be given an honorable burial.

The final scene shows fellow gladiator and friend Juba (Djion Hounsou) burying the carved figures Maximus had kept with him. Juba speaks to Maximus, saying, "Now we are free." He closes by telling him he will see him again. "But not yet. Not yet."

Notice how all of the subplots and each of the questions raised in the first act are answered in the outcome of the final battle and the denouement that follows it. A great ending.

So how might you go about writing a great denouement on the way to writing a great ending? Here are some suggestions:

- First, do not decide on your denouement until after you have written several drafts of the script and understand everything you are trying to say with your film. Do not be afraid to change what you have already written as a denouement, even if it seemed "right" the first time through.

- Whenever you decide, remember to examine all of your subplots to make sure that they have all been resolved. If not, you must do so somewhere in the denouement.

- If your main character has a stated desire that is different from the question you raised at the end of the first act, make sure that the question concerning that desire is answered somewhere in the denouement.

- If the outcome of the final battle creates a negative feeling or impression, be sure to include at least one scene in the denouement to help alleviate that feeling, if appropriate.

- If you are writing a comedy, consider a curtain call, which will be welcomed by the audience (and give you a chance for one more laugh).

- Finally, if your story has a theme and it can be reinforced without being heavy-handed, consider a scene or scenes that will do so just prior to fading to black.

Chapter Eight

The Bridge

So far we have examined the four essential elements of a strong third act on the way to a great ending. However, earlier, I mentioned a fifth element that is sometimes part of that structure and often essential to creating that great ending.

I call this element "the bridge."

The name comes about because this scene or these scenes act to connect the outcome of the final battle to the last scene or action of the main character. It is used whenever the writer and/or the filmmaker feels that some explanation is required in order for the reader/audience to fully understand and appreciate what is to follow after the outcome of the final battle. Most often, it helps to explain *why* the main character is doing what they are doing in the film's final scene or scenes.

You'll notice that this element involves explanation, which is just another word for "exposition," as that term is used in screenwriting. Anytime anything is "explained" in a movie, it is "exposition." But, despite what you may have read or heard, exposition is not a dirty word. Some screenwriting instructors speak of exposition as if it is something to be avoided when writing a screenplay. Not true. What these critics really object to is *bad* exposition, or exposition that is so obvious as to call attention to itself.

Every script/movie requires some exposition. Otherwise, we may not fully understand or appreciate what we are seeing. Good writers write exposition in such a way as to make it appear natural and unobtrusive. And the same goes for "the bridge," which is a specific bit of exposition that (sometimes) occurs in the third act, following the outcome of the final battle.

Note that exposition coming so late in a film is rare. In normal circumstances, any information that the audience needs in order to fully understand and appreciate the story will likely have to be given long before the third act. And especially long before the outcome of the final battle. Heck, by the time we get there, we *better* understand what's going on. But there are exceptions, which is what this chapter is all about.

Again, let me emphasize that not all scripts/films require a bridge. In fact, most don't. But there are times when it is necessary for us to fully comprehend and appreciate the ending.

Let's look at some of the films we have talked about so far where there is *no* bridge and discuss why that is so.

(1) *Rocky*

As you recall, the outcome of the final battle (the fight) is that Rocky lasts the entire fifteen rounds. In the denouement that follows, we learn that Rocky has lost the fight in a split decision. In the midst of this announcement, Rocky calls for Adrian, not even caring about the judges' decision. Adrian, with the help of her brother, Paulie, manages to sneak into the ring where she and Rocky embrace and express their love for one another. We freeze on their embrace. The end.

Since the final shot is that of Rocky and Adrian embracing, there is no need for any explanation. They are not strangers. We know they love one another. Nothing that occurs in the final battle or the denouement makes the final action of our main character confusing or difficult to accept. No need for a bridge here.

(2) *Saving Private Ryan*

At the end of the (literal) final battle, James Ryan is "saved" but Captain Miller dies. In the previous chapter, we examined the denouement, which consists almost entirely of a return to the present day and the older Ryan at the cemetery in France. As we discussed, he asks his wife if he has been a good man and whether he has lived a good life, all prompted by Miller's plea to him before he dies. Ryan's wife assures James that he has lived a good life and is a good man. That's it.

Nowhere in those scenes does anything occur that requires an explanation. Our feelings following the battle are not in danger of changing. There is no risk of the older Ryan acting in any way that might be misinterpreted or misunderstood. In fact, we are not surprised when he asks the question, nor are we caught off-guard by his wife's answer. More important, our main character is dead. Thus, there is no chance that we will misinterpret any later action by him, because there can be no later action by him. Simply put, there is no need for a bridge here.

(3) *Gladiator*

At the conclusion of the fight in the arena, Commodus dies. But so does Maximus a short time later. As he does, we see through his eyes his long-awaited "reunion" with his family. Once that occurs, we next see him lifeless on the floor of the arena, his body respectfully removed by Roman soldiers and gladiators. Thereafter, we see Juba, Maximus's gladiator friend, bury the carved figures representing Maximus's family, and we learn that this friend will be returning to his family as well.

Nothing that occurs after the outcome of the final battle (or the "reunion") requires an explanation. There is no danger that what next occurs will be misunderstood. In fact, as in *Saving Private Ryan*, our main character is gone. His final act was to die, which requires no exposition. No need for a bridge in this story either.

(4) *Witness*

The outcome of our final battle in this film is that Schaeffer, the corrupt police lieutenant, is prevented from killing Book or Samuel by the presence of the Amish "witnesses."

Thereafter, we see (but don't hear) Book talking with the police who have arrived at the Lapp farm to clean up the mess. This scene is followed by Book and Samuel sitting beside the pond. Next, we have Book and Rachel looking at one another on the porch.

After Eli's friendly warning to Book, the last scene is Book in his car driving away from the farm, stopping to say something to Hochleitner. The frame freezes and credits roll.

Nothing that follows Schaeffer's capture (outcome of the final battle) requires an explanation. Nor are Book's actions after that in any way in danger of being misinterpreted. Or are they?

There may be some who think some words should have been exchanged between Book and Rachel on that porch to "explain" why he was leaving. And as mentioned in the previous chapter, an earlier version of the script did just that. And that was a bridge scene. For it "explained" why Book was not staying at the farm or, perhaps, why Rachel wasn't going with him.

But as we discussed previously, was this really necessary? Peter Weir didn't think so. And so he took out all dialogue between the two, believing that we in the audience did not require an explanation for why Book was leaving alone. I think this was a wise choice. Why? Remember that earlier, in act two, Book did not respond to Rachel's rather obvious invitation to become intimate with her when she was standing half-naked before him while bathing. The next day, Book "explained" to Rachel that if he had done so, she would have to leave with him or he'd have to stay. The implication was that both were aware that neither of those options could happen.

So when Rachel came to Book the night before the "final battle" and they embraced in the sunset out in the field, we can only assume she was telling him that it was okay. That neither of those two things would have to happen after they became intimate. They could simply share their feelings and go back to their separate lives. At the end, their smiles and silence on the porch merely reaffirms this. In sum, while the writers may have thought such a scene might be necessary, it turned out that we do not need a bridge to understand the final actions of John Book.

Now let's compare those films with some we have discussed that do contain a "bridge" and examine the difference.

(1) *Good Will Hunting*

Will's breakthrough in Sean's office is the outcome of the final battle. Everything that follows is the denouement, which is long and varied because of the number of subplots. We examined the resolution of each of those subplots in the previous chapter. But we did not discuss one series of scenes accompanied by Will's voiceover.

Will takes the car given to him by his friends for his twenty-first birthday (ironically, the means by which he will leave them) and drives to Sean's apartment to leave him a note. We cut back and forth between the scenes of Chuck waiting outside Will's door for Will to come out and Sean packing for his impending trip back at his apartment.

We then see Sean finding the note outside his apartment. Over this scene and the ones where Chuck realizes that Will is not in his apartment (fulfilling Chuck's wish), Will reads the note.

Sean provides the final line of the film ("Son of a bitch, he stole my line"). And then we see the final shot of Will driving away on the Massachusetts Turnpike heading for California and, we presume, Skyler.

The scenes of Will delivering the note and the voiceover that follows make up the bridge. Why?

Imagine for a moment that these scenes and the accompanying voiceover are not included and all we see is the final shot of Will driving down the Turnpike at the end. What happens?

Chuck has gone to Will's apartment only to find him gone. Sean is most likely not shown at all, or if he is, he is simply packing for the trip we already know about. And we wonder: where the heck Will is going? And why? What about that job in Boston? He told Sean he was taking it. What does his sudden departure mean? Is he running away? Has the "breakthrough" caused him to leave *everything* behind? Without the note and voiceover, we simply would not know.

The scene of Will driving down the Turnpike at the very end of the movie demands some explanation in order for us to completely understand and appreciate what has happened to Will as a result of the outcome of the final battle (the breakthrough).

Voiceover is exposition. Exposition is explanation. Explanation at this point in the third act is a bridge to the final action of the main character. In this film it is Will's departure. Without that bridge, the third act would not work nearly as well as it does.

(2) *Cast Away*

Remember the outcome of the final battle? Chuck leaves Kelly's home with the realization that they can no longer be together. Quite a downer. For Chuck and us.

In the previous chapter, we discussed the denouement. In particular, we focused on Chuck's trip to deliver the package. We see him leave the note for the woman at the ranch. We then see Chuck at the crossroads (literally). We watch the woman return and stop to give Chuck some directions. And we watch Chuck watch the woman drive down the road toward that ranch, thinking that he will soon follow her. But why do we think that?

Because of the "bridge" scene that occurs just prior to this series of scenes.

This scene is the one immediately following Chuck's departure from Kelly's house. Recall that Chuck has a middle-of-the-night chat with Stan, his coworker from FedEx. In this chat, Chuck tells Stan about almost committing suicide on the island and then regaining hope and wanting to save himself when the wind blew in the "sail" he later used on the raft that took him from the island.

Chuck tells Stan (and us) that Kelly was his motivation for leaving. He tells his friend (and us) how sad he is that she has now moved on. But he also tells him (and us) that he knows he can go on because "you never know what the tide will bring." Pure exposition. In fact, Stan never says a word. This scene is just Chuck telling us (explaining) his feelings both on the island and after seeing Kelly earlier that evening.

In the series of scenes that follow, we see what the tide has brought in for Chuck: that woman on the ranch. Which is why we know he will drive up that road after her. Without that bridge scene, would we really accept Chuck going after that woman? Without knowing that he has that renewed faith, would we accept this action of Chuck at the very end? Maybe. But it would be difficult. And more than one in the audience might think he has gotten over Kelly pretty quickly. Which we know is not the case after watching the bridge scene. Its use here is masterful and necessary.

(3) *Rain Man*

We have not talked about the four elements of the third act of *Rain Man* in the previous chapters, so let's review them here.

After journeying across the country, Charlie returns safely to L.A. with Raymond (second-act plot point). Once there, he moves Raymond into his Hollywood Hills home (preparation for the final battle). Charlie meets later that night with Dr. Bruner, the doctor from Wallbrook, and Bruner offers Charlie a check for $250,000 as payment for Charlie dropping his lawsuit to gain custody of Raymond (more preparation). Charlie refuses the money (more preparation). The next morning Raymond nearly burns down Charlie's house when he tries to make waffles in the toaster oven (more preparation). Raymond takes Charlie out for a pancake breakfast and they make a joke and a connection (even more preparation).

The pair then appear at the office of Doctor Morrison, the court-appointed psychiatrist (played by director Barry Levinson) who is to examine Raymond in anticipation of the court battle over custody. This is the final battle. After asking some questions about their weeklong journey from Ohio to L.A., the doctor questions Raymond's ability to make a decision about where he would like to live. Charlie disagrees strongly, saying he knows more about Raymond than either doctor. Charlie urges Morrison to ask Raymond his preference.

The doctor promptly does so. And the scene plays out splendidly when we hear Raymond say that he wants to stay in L.A. with Charlie Babbitt. However, when Doctor Morrison asks Raymond if he wants to go back to Wallbrook, Raymond says yes to that as well. The doctor asks Raymond which of the two he wants. In response, Raymond simply repeats both things over and over until it is clear that Raymond cannot make the decision, forcing Charlie to concede that Raymond would be better off living under the supervision provided at Wallbrook (outcome of the final battle).

The final scenes in the film show Charlie seeing Raymond off at the train station bound for Ohio with Doctor Bruner accompanying him. Before he leaves, we hear Charlie tell Raymond that just because he doesn't have custody doesn't mean that he can't see him. In fact, he's coming out in three weeks. It's a nice moment.

Except that we have witnessed Charlie lie throughout this film. It is almost his default mode. Can we really accept that Charlie will visit Raymond and maintain a relationship with his brother?

Not likely without the bridge scene that happens just prior to this one.

That scene occurs in the doctor's office right after Raymond's stay-in-L.A./go-back-to-Wallbrook moment. Both doctors step out of the office, leaving Charlie and Raymond alone. Charlie then explains to his brother that he meant everything that he said to the doctors moments before. He *has* changed (as we suspect). He has made a connection with his brother. He's glad to have Raymond for a big brother. There is no need for Charlie to lie here. Nothing is at stake. They are alone. His words are heartfelt and we believe him.

Which is why we accept Charlie's claim at the train station that he will be going out to see his brother in three weeks. And why we think it is genuine. Without that "bridge" scene in the office one scene earlier, we might have doubts. (More on **Rain Man** in a later chapter.)

Now, after looking at all of those examples, you might feel that the "bridge" scene is just another scene in the denouement. No more. No less. And it would be hard to argue, especially if you accept the definition of the denouement as "everything that follows the outcome of the final battle."

However, the "bridge" scene is unique in that it is expository in nature while most scenes in a denouement have no such requirement. In fact, exposition is rarely required at the end of a movie. It is this specific purpose that calls for it to be singled out and considered separately from the rest of the denouement. While it is not *always* necessary for it to be included in every third act, there are times when it is called for in order to create the great ending you desire.

How might you know when is it necessary in your script?

Again, it is story-dependent. But some things to look for when considering whether to use a "bridge" scene:

- Will the audience accept the final action(s) of your main character without some explanation?
- Can the audience fully understand and appreciate what will happen to your main character after the outcome of the final battle?
- Do the actions of any other character, in the aid of your main character, require some clarification before the film can end?

If you find yourself uncomfortable about some aspect of your denouement, you may want to consider a "bridge" scene to help the reader/audience fully appreciate your ending.

Chapter Nine

Endings

The stated purpose of this book is to help you achieve a great ending for your script. But before I go any further, it might be helpful to define the term "ending" as it applies to both a script and a film.

So how do we do so? How do we go about defining a movie's "ending"?

First, let's test the hypothesis that endings and a moviegoer's evaluation of a film are inexorably linked. Ask your moviegoing friends about some movies they have seen recently. In each case, ask whether they "loved" the movie or not. Separate those that they loved from those that they did not. Then ask if they liked the "ending" of each.

I would bet that if they "loved" a movie, they at least "liked" the "ending." And just as likely, if they did not "love" a movie, they did not "like" the "ending." It is certainly possible to like an ending, but dislike a film. Rare, but not impossible. However, I believe it is almost unheard of for a person to love the film and dislike the ending. Feel free to test this hypothesis.

Let's take it a step further now. With respect to either category, ask them to describe "the ending."

Okay, what did you get? Assuming you've seen the movie and can analyze the third act according to the structure laid out in this book, I am going to predict that when you break down their description you will find that what they call the "ending" consists of a combination of "the outcome of the final battle" and part or all of "the denouement."

I am just as confident that they will not describe the "ending" as simply the final scene or shot of the film. If they do, then ask them why they call that the "ending." Or better yet, ask them how that "ends" the film.

Once again, I am certain that they will then proceed to tell you some additional information, not contained in that final shot or scene. And that additional information will almost certainly include the outcome of the final battle and, perhaps, some additional portion of the denouement.

If you think about it for a moment, it makes perfect sense. The outcome of the final battle answers the question raised at the end of the first act. That's what the audience longs to find out as they watch the film. And if that question is the same as the main character's external desire, well, the outcome answers that as well. But that's only part of the "ending," isn't it?

If you accept one of the definitions I gave earlier, that the denouement is the main character's and/or the world's response to the outcome of the final battle, then that response is essential to understanding and appreciating the outcome of the final battle.

If the denouement serves other purposes in addition to presenting the response to the outcome of the final battle, it is likely that one of those purposes might be an answer to the question posed by the main character's internal desire. And even if it is simply a curtain call, that is likely to be the ensemble's response to the outcome of the final battle.

Regardless, it is almost certain that neither the outcome of the final battle alone nor the denouement by itself can comprise what the viewer would consider the film's "ending."

Let's see how this works with some of the films we have been talking about thus far.

(1) *Rocky*

If you were to ask a friend to describe the ending of **Rocky**, they would probably say something like this: Rocky goes the distance with Apollo Creed, but he doesn't win the fight, and he's okay with that because he ends up with Adrian.

Notice that this description includes the outcome of the final battle (Rocky lasts the full fifteen rounds) and most of the denouement (he loses the fight, but ends up in Adrian's arms).

Anything less than this doesn't do the "ending" justice, does it? Is your friend likely to say only that Rocky ends up with Adrian but never mention the fight or its outcome?

On the other hand, are they likely to say only that Rocky lasts the full fifteen rounds, but not mention that he *lost the fight*? They may leave out Adrian, but they won't leave out the fact that Rocky lost the fight. And I would wager that they would say both. After all, that final shot of Rocky and Adrian is as memorable as they come.

(2) *Good Will Hunting*

Ask that same friend about the "ending" of this movie and you are likely to hear that Will gets over his past, in which he was an abused child, and leaves Boston to go after the girl.

Again, this description takes into account the outcome of the final battle (he gets over his past) and part of the denouement (he leaves Boston and goes after Skyler).

If they were to simply say that he goes after the girl, then ask them why he does so. The chances are more than pretty good that they will tell you that he does so *because he has overcome the problems of his past.*

By the same token, they are unlikely to say that the "ending" is that Will gets over his childhood without mentioning what he does in response to that occurrence.

First of all, the scene of him driving away in the car is simply too memorable and symbolic of him leaving his past behind. Second, the entire sequence of Chuck appearing at Will's doorstep and Sean receiving Will's note is likewise too important to the story to be dismissed or left out when describing to someone how the movie ends.

As with **Rocky**, most viewers would likely describe the ending of this film by noting the outcome of the main character's final battle and his response thereto.

(3) *Cast Away*

As we discussed in an earlier chapter, it's possible that your friend may not like the "ending" to this movie. Why?

Well, if you ask them what the "ending" was, they will no doubt tell you that Chuck gets rescued after five years on the island only to return and find Kelly married to someone else, thereby preventing them from getting back together. Which just happens to be the outcome of the final battle.

But they are not likely to stop there. However, if they do, then ask if that's all that happens at the end. Undoubtedly, they will say no, and then inform you that Chuck ends up delivering a package to some attractive woman down in Texas who (it appears at least) he is going follow up the road.

It is highly unlikely that they would simply tell you about the woman at the end without ever mentioning Kelly. And they most likely will not tell you about Chuck's realization about Kelly's unavailability without adding the final scene at the end of the film, because this scene keeps the "ending" from being a complete downer.

Once more, we have the outcome of the final battle with a portion of the denouement making up the "ending."

(4) *Witness*

Anyone describing the ending of this film would likely say that John Book manages to save Samuel from the corrupt Philadelphia cops. They might even go so far as to get specific about how he did so, acknowledging the role of the Amish in preventing Schaeffer from doing any harm to Samuel or Book or Rachel.

But because the romance subplot is so essential to the story, taking up a huge portion of the second act, it is likely also that they would have to mention that Book does not stay on the farm and returns to Philadelphia without Rachel.

It could be argued that both of those occurrences are such memorable scenes that a casual viewer might name one and neglect the other in explaining the ending. But I doubt it. To concentrate on the romance aspect without noting that Book actually protected Samuel would do a disservice to the whole point of the film. And to mention only the outcome of the final battle (Schaeffer's surrender) would leave out one of the main characters (Rachel) and the strongest subplot. Book's leaving and Rachel's staying is the resolution to that subplot, as well as his (and her) reaction to the outcome of the final battle.

(5) *Gladiator*

No doubt, anyone explaining the ending to this film would begin with Maximus killing Commodus in the arena. After all, it is a certain outcome to a literal battle in a movie involving lots of battles. And that might be all that one would say. Unless asked what happens to Maximus.

At that point, I have no doubt that they would mention that Maximus also dies and goes to see his family in the afterlife. Because that scene in the denouement is so vivid and unusual, I think the casual viewer would be unlikely to omit it from any discussion about this film's ending. Notice, though, that this scene is only part of the denouement. I would probably concede that very few would mention the return of Rome to a republic. This seems almost to be an afterthought and of less interest to the audience.

On the other hand, Juba's burial of the wooden figures that Maximus carried with him representing his wife and son might merit mention by someone describing the ending. Once again, this is a vivid and memorable scene. But if that were all they said in explaining the ending, a simple question of what happened to Maximus would bring about their mention of all of the above.

However you look at it, any description of the "ending" of this film must involve the outcome of the final battle (Maximus kills Commodus) and some part of the denouement.

(6) *Saving Private Ryan*

This movie also contains some memorable scenes at the end. I have no way of confirming this next statement, short of scientific polling, but I believe the vast majority of those who saw this movie would describe the "ending" as consisting of the scene at the cemetery in Normandy involving the elder James Ryan and his wife. But if someone were to tell you that was the "ending," you might then ask them how Ryan happens to be alive to visit that cemetery with his wife, children, and grandchildren. At that point, they would have to tell you about the scene on the bridge and Captain Miller's heroic death, which helped to "save" private Ryan. Indeed, the cemetery scene (denouement) would not even occur without the outcome of the final battle. Thus, any discussion about the "ending" of this film would have to include both.

Looking at these examples, my conclusion is that audiences may often describe a film's final scene or scenes when explaining the ending. But upon further inquiry, they would then have to concede that those scenes would never have come about without that which precedes them. And that which precedes them, invariably, is the outcome of the final battle.

Are there exceptions to this?

Sure. In fact, the shorter the denouement, the more likely that the "ending" will be described simply as the outcome of the final battle. Two examples of this would be **Thelma & Louise** and **Butch Cassidy and the Sundance Kid.** With respect to the former, we already discussed the last scene, which is the two women going over the edge of the Grand Canyon in that convertible. This is as memorable as a final scene can be. And the denouement is simply a brief retrospective of earlier (and happier) scenes.

As for **Butch Cassidy**, there is likewise a memorable final scene. And that, of course, is the one in which Butch and Sundance burst out of the cantina with guns blazing, only to be met with a barrage of fire from the assembled Bolivian army. This is clearly the outcome of the final battle, even though the frame freezes and we don't see the bullets actually striking the pair. We don't need to. We know what is going to happen. So what about the denouement?

It is there, albeit brief. In my opinion, the scene transition from a color freeze-frame to the sepia-toned photograph serves as a denouement. Why? I would submit that this photograph serves to inform us of the legendary characters that Butch and Sundance became. And this is the world's response to the outcome of the final battle. While it is certainly short, it is also quite effective, and it helps to alleviate any sorrowful feelings we might have upon (almost) seeing their demise.

One might say the same thing about **Thelma & Louise**. In the director's notes accompanying the DVD of this film, director Ridley Scott explained that he considered (and filmed) a scene of the car actually landing on the canyon floor. But he rejected that "ending," believing that the visual image of that car suspended in air helped to keep these women "alive" and bestowed upon them a "legendary" status, similar to Butch and Sundance.

One can take this comparison to **Butch Cassidy** even further by noting that just before their car disappears over the canyon rim, we see a picture of Thelma & Louise taken before the trip blow out of the car. Though this film is obviously fiction, the idea was to make these women live on after their death, just like the real Butch and Sundance. The snapshot helps to do that.

Note that it requires some pretty skillful writing to get away with such a short denouement and still create a "great ending." Other films have attempted to "end" with the outcome of the final battle while providing little or no denouement (the 2003 film **Seabiscuit**, written and directed by Gary Ross, comes to mind here). That would obviously lead one to describe the "ending" as merely the outcome of the final battle. But I would argue that if that is the case, it is also likely that the person who describes the "ending" in such a fashion might also tell you they felt that something was missing. Why? Simple. We all want to see what effect the outcome of the final battle has had on our main character and/or the world. And that is what the denouement does for us.

But, remember that's not all we want. We want a "great ending." And that means a *memorable* response to a *memorable* outcome. So how do we achieve that, using the outcome of the final battle and at least a portion of the denouement?

William Goldman says great endings are both "satisfying and surprising." Robert McKee tells us that Aristotle posited that great endings are both "inevitable and unexpected." (Actually, depending on the interpretation, Aristotle recommended endings that are "contrary to one's expectation" and "as if on purpose." They are one and the same in my mind, and so it is hard to argue with McKee's choice of words.)

Regardless of which of those two definitions you choose (Goldman versus Aristotle), finding the right combination of the outcome of the final battle and the response thereto poses a difficult task for you the writer. There is no one correct way to do that. As you have heard me say throughout this book, it is story-dependent.

The best I can offer are some things to keep in mind as you develop your story. Or, if you have already written it, some things to look at in your draft to see if they are present and fulfill their purpose(s).

- Have you adequately prepared your final battle by selecting an obstacle that is greater than all others faced by your main character so far in the story?
- Have you made certain to arrange it so that your main character ends up one-on-one with his/her greatest villain or opposing force in that final battle?
- Have you made certain that the battle he/she engages in with that villain or obstacle is such that he/she faces enor-

mous odds in his/her attempt to overcome that person or obstacle?

- Have you staged your final battle so as to wring the maximum amount of drama (or comedy) out of that confrontation?
- Does the outcome of your final battle answer the question raised at the end of the first act?
- If your main character's stated desire is not the same as that question, do you provide an answer to that desire in your denouement?
- Have you adequately shown your main character's response to the outcome of the final battle?
- If appropriate, have you adequately shown the world's response to the outcome of the final battle?
- Have you examined whether you might need a "bridge" scene to "explain" the actions of your main character following the outcome of the final battle?
- Have you examined whether you might need a "bridge" scene to insure that the audience will fully understand and appreciate the theme of your story?
- Have you written your denouement so that the "ending" can be easily understood and described by the reader/audience?

In a later chapter, we'll examine the "endings" of some recent films that merited some critical acclaim, were written by skilled screenwriters and directed by award-winning directors, but were not received as well as anticipated. For the most part, they were shut out of the major awards in their respective years of release, despite all of that talent on board. And the reason for that, in my opinion, may very well be those "endings."

However, before we do that, let's look at...

Chapter Ten

The Three Hs: Hollywood,
Happy, and Hopeful

So far, we have taken a structural approach to creating "great" endings. And we have defined the term "ending" in a way that is compatible with our intended audience. But what we haven't yet discussed is the "type" of ending that you might create in your efforts to come up with a "great" one.

The "type" of ending can mean just about anything. But mostly when people talk about endings they do so in general terms. Thus, an ending can be categorized as an "up" ending or a "down" ending, those terms being rather self-explanatory. And generic.

An even more common terminology employed is the "happy" ending, which seems to imply something more than just an "up" ending. Nearly synonymous with the "happy" ending is the time-worn "Hollywood" ending.

Like the happy ending, the Hollywood ending seems to imply more than an "up" ending. But it also seems to go a bit farther than "happy," as if those who are responsible for making films in Hollywood want to sugarcoat or sweeten the endings of their films beyond the simple emotion of happiness.

And there is no doubt some support for that claim, at least

when we examine Hollywood's past. Certainly, during difficult times in our nation's history, Hollywood has made films that seemed designed to lift the spirits of the entire country. Even today, there are some films that appear to take the route of attempting to send the audience out of the theater on a high. Who hasn't read a review or blurb that claims that the advertised film will "have the audience on their feet cheering"?

In 2003, we had *Seabiscuit*, an Academy Award Nominee for Best Picture and Best Screenplay. In 2005, we had another depression-era film in *Cinderella Man*. Both are based on true- life stories and each was somewhat restricted by the historical record. But in both instances, the filmmakers made choices to feature endings in the old Hollywood tradition. It is probably not a coincidence that both stories take place at a time when our country was in need of a boost, both economically and sociologically.

But I would argue that an examination of some of Hollywood's most beloved and best films do not have a sugarcoated ending. Not by a long stretch. Which doesn't necessarily mean that all in Hollywood have rejected the "happy" ending. As the list below demonstrates, it is alive and well.

Still, there is a breed of ending that Hollywood and audiences seem to embrace, and it is neither "Hollywood" in the traditional sense, nor "happy." In fact, it falls somewhere short of "happy" and far short of "Hollywood." I call this the "hopeful" ending. And in your quest to write a "great" ending, it is one you should consider for your script, if appropriate.

Don't misunderstand me here. Not all "great" endings are "hopeful." Nor are all "hopeful" endings "great." It just so happens that "hopeful" endings tend to be more satisfying than either "Hollywood" or "happy" endings for certain types of films. And, as William Goldman advises, we as an audience look for a measure of satisfaction at the end of our movie-watching experience.

Before going on to describe the "hopeful" ending and provide some examples, it might be helpful to look at some films that have

"Hollywood" and/or "happy" endings. Since there is often a negative connotation to those terms, you might be surprised at some of the films on this list.

(1) *It's a Wonderful Life*

George won't be going to prison, he's learned to appreciate his family and friends, and staying in Bedford Falls won't be as much of a sacrifice after Clarence's Christmas Eve visit.

(2) *The Philadelphia Story*

The divorced couple that should never have gotten divorced in the first place wind up remarrying at the end.

(3) *The Apartment*

The poor schlub who lent his apartment to his superiors for their afternoon and evening trysts ends up with the ultimate prize: his boss's mistress.

(4) *Jaws*

The guy who hates the water kills the shark and saves his island community. (At least until the sequel.)

(5) *Moonstruck*

The bad-luck heroine ends up marrying the right brother, for love instead of comfort.

(6) *My Big Fat Greek Wedding*

The ugly duckling ends up marrying the handsome nonethnic fellow. And not only that, they move next door to her crazy family! And without a peep from the husband! Only in Hollywood!

(7) *Jerry Maguire*

The commitment-phobic sports agent ends up with a business he can be proud of and a pretty cool wife and stepson to boot!

(8) *Notting Hill*

The underachieving bookstore owner ends up marrying the most famous actress in the world. And his googly-eyed sister ends up with his wacky roommate on top of it!

(9) *Pretty Woman*

The reluctant call girl ends up with the rich and handsome corporate executive. Say no more.

(10) *The African Queen*

The reformed alcoholic and the straight-laced missionary find common ground, marriage, and, oh yeah, manage to sink a German warship all in a few days time.

Again, don't get me wrong. These are all good, if not great, films (though I might quibble a bit on *My Big Fat Greek Wedding* and *Pretty Woman*). Yet they all feature a "happy" ending. Notice that there are more than a few that are either romantic comedies or involve romance on some level.

But what is it that makes them "happy"?

Generally, a "happy" ending is one in which the main character achieves his stated desire, so long as that is a positive thing, or, if you prefer, "up." (There is yet another category of happy ending, although I will save any discussion of that for chapter 11.)

What about "unhappy" endings? Is there such a thing and, if so, can a movie have such an ending and still be considered "great"? In a word, yes. Still, that ending must "satisfy" the audience, which is no small task.

Here's a look at some films with endings that could be called "unhappy."

(1) *The Graduate*

Ben gets the girl, but the look on their faces on that bus in the last shot does not leave us feeling very optimistic about he and

Katherine. Plus, she's probably going to have to get the marriage annulled at the very least.

(2) *Sunset Boulevard*

The poor struggling screenwriter is dead at the end. Never a good thing.

(3) *American Beauty*

The newly fit and buff Lester Burnham ends up dead (though he seems okay with that).

(4) *Chinatown*

The ultimate downer for many people. Jake Gitties solves the case, but his new girlfriend (and incest victim) ends up dead.

(5) *Thelma & Louise*

Like Lester, they both end up dead. Heck of a ride, though.

(6) *Butch Cassidy and the Sundance Kid*

Both dead. But at least we didn't have to see it. Instead, they live on in our memory. Not to mention AMC.

(7) *The Godfather*

Michael kills everyone who is against him and then lies to his wife about it when it's all over.

(8) *Easy Rider*

Once more, both dead. Heck of a ride again.

(9) *Unforgiven*

Revenge. But hardly sweet.

(10) *Million Dollar Baby*

Assisted suicide. Say no more.

Now you'll notice there are more than a few Academy Award winners in that group, both for Best Picture and Screenplay. Who says Hollywood likes a "happy" ending? Notice also that, except for **The Graduate**, every one of those involves a death in the outcome of the final battle. Hardly surprising since death is generally an unhappy event.

Which brings us back to that middle category that I like to call the "hopeful" ending. This ending leaves us feeling that the main character has come out of their ordeal intact, but not at the top of the world. Still, there is a bit of hope on the horizon for him or her.

One of the more satisfying features of hopeful endings is that they don't resolve everything in the main character's life. They aren't a lottery win. But they aren't assisted suicide either. We walk out of the theater thinking that things will probably work out for the main character, if not forever, then at least for the near term. And who among us wouldn't take that in our own lives? In fact, that is part of their appeal, in my judgment. "Hope" at the end of a particularly difficult ordeal is far more realistic to expect than "happy," for most of us anyway. Which, oddly, is more satisfying to a discerning audience.

Here is look at some films that feature "hopeful" endings.

(1) *Rain Man*

Charlie doesn't end up with his father's money. Or even the $250,000 check that Doctor Bruner offered him. Which means that those cars he imported will probably end up bankrupting him. But he has an older brother that he never knew he had. Not bad.

(2) *The Shawshank Redemption*

Andy never gets to prove his innocence. He isn't pardoned. The conviction remains on the books. And they're probably out looking for him, despite the warden's suicide. But at least he's not in prison anymore. And his best friend has just joined him on the beach, an entire continent away.

(3) *The Fabulous Baker Boys*

Jeff Bridges won't be working the hotel circuit with brother Beau anymore. He'll probably make less money at that little jazz club where he's going to play. But Michelle Pfeiffer appears to have forgiven him. That's pretty hopeful to me.

(4) *Titanic*

Jack dies in those icy waters. Rose doesn't have much longer herself. But she's lived a pretty darn good life, all thanks to Jack. We don't see her going out with any regrets.

(5) *Casablanca*

Rick lets the love of his life get on that plane to Lisbon. He's also sold his fabulously successful nightclub. And he's about to go on the run with Captain Renault. But somehow things are still looking up for him.

(6) *Ghost*

She finally has to let go of her dead husband. But they're both going to be okay now. (Hey, there's an afterlife!)

(7) *Tootsie*

Michael isn't exactly picking up any starring roles on Broadway or Hollywood. But he does break the ice with Jessica Lange. She hasn't exactly said yes. But if you had to guess...

(8) *Almost Famous*

Patrick doesn't get the girl. But he does get the cover of the *Rolling Stone*. And enough stories to last a lifetime.

(9) *Cast Away*

Speaking of getting the girl, it's not Kelly, but that woman in Texas is pretty cute, too. As in *Tootsie*, she hasn't said yes yet, but if you had to bet...

(10) *Some Like It Hot*

The gangsters aren't chasing them anymore. They no longer need to wear women's clothes. But Jack Lemmon has found himself a sugar daddy. (Nobody's perfect.)

The point of this is that your story doesn't have to have a happy ending to be great. If it does and it works, all the better. But an "unhappy" ending might work just as well, depending on your characters and your theme. And there is a third option, the hopeful ending where your main character survives his greatest ordeal, things look generally positive, though he or she may still have a ways to go.

How you decide on the type of ending is entirely up to you. But looking closely at your main character's desire will go a long way toward helping you decide. Likewise, examining the consequences of giving your main character exactly what he or she wants may make your choice a little easier.

Which leads us to yet another choice for an ending. This is one that I like to call...

Chapter Eleven

Something Better

You will remember that the outcome of the final battle must relate back and answer the question you raised at the end of the first act. Note also that the answer to this question must be unequivocal. The reader/audience must be satisfied that whatever was in doubt at the end of the first act is no longer in doubt.

The same holds true for the question raised by your main character's stated desire, assuming that stated desire is different from the question raised at the end of the first act.

However, just because you have to remove all doubt when answering those questions does not mean that you have to resolve all of the issues in your main character's life. You do not need to wrap up everything in your character's life in a nice package with a fancy ribbon. In fact, there are times when you can put a twist on the answer(s) you provide in your ending.

We talked in the previous chapter about Hollywood endings, happy endings, unhappy endings, and even hopeful ones. They all have their use and any one of them can make for a "great ending." But there is a particular kind of hopeful ending that we haven't yet discussed and this one often works to great effect.

I call it "something better."

Simply put, this ending applies when your main character wants something and doesn't get it. That's right—they don't get what they want! Compare this to the pure happy ending, where that is precisely what occurs—your main character overcomes the obstacles and achieves the object of his or her desire.

With the "something better" ending, your main character doesn't achieve the object of their desire but, in a satisfying twist, they get "something better." Often, the "something" they get is a thing that they did not even contemplate nor consider at the start of the film. And just as often, it is something that they subconsciously wanted but never allowed themselves to wish for.

So why does this "twist" work?

Generally speaking, with this type of ending, after living with the main character throughout the movie, we come to feel that they should not get the object of their desire. It simply would not be right for the character or us as an audience.

Now it may not be a conscious feeling on our part as we watch the movie. But when the film is over and we think about it, we are certain that what they have gotten at the end of the movie is far superior to what they originally said they wanted. Moreover, we are certain that they must now realize the same thing. This ending is both satisfying and surprising, which, after all, is what we seek from an ending in the first place.

Let's examine four films that end in this fashion and see why they satisfy us.

(1) *Casablanca*

The questions raised at the end of the first act are: what will Rick do with those exit visas? And, to a lesser extent, what is his past connection with Ilsa? (Somehow we know the two will be connected.)

However, recall that Rick's stated desire is to "stick his neck out for no man." In other words, Rick wants to remain neutral. But not just in any circumstances. Here in Casablanca, in the midst of the greatest battle between right and wrong—those who desire freedom versus the Nazis seeking world domination—Rick wants to remain on the sidelines.

In the third act, we get an unequivocal answer to the question raised at the end of the first act: Rick uses those exit visas to allow Ilsa and her husband Victor Laszlo to escape Casablanca after Rick reconciles his bitter feelings for Ilsa having left him in Paris years before. Not only that, but in Rick's doing so we also get an unequivocal answer regarding his stated desire. He will no longer remain neutral. He will stick his neck out. Way out. How? By shooting and killing Major Strasser, the highest-ranking German officer in Casablanca, thereby assuring that Ilsa and Victor can make a safe departure.

Rick doesn't get what he wants (neutrality). He gets "something better": closure with Ilsa and a reaffirmation of his belief that good should never give in to evil.

It is important to note here that we see a hint of this side of Rick before the third act. It comes when Rick allows the Austrian couple to win at roulette so as to avoid the wife having to sleep with Captain Renault in order to get an exit visa. This shows us that this belief that good should triumph over evil has always been inside Rick. But it has been suppressed in recent years because of a severely broken heart. This scene lets us know that Rick really wants to do the right thing and take a stand against evil and/or wrongdoing.

In the ending, this desire emerges completely. And Rick is better off than he was at the beginning of the movie, even though he has had to abandon both the love of his life and his friends and business in Casablanca. We know this for sure. And now, so does Rick.

(2) *Rain Man*

The question at the end of the first act in **Rain Man** is a simple one: will Charlie Babbitt successfully gain custody of his newly discovered and autistic older brother so that he can gain access to the money in the estate of his deceased father (money he needs to get the imported cars rebuilt and sold)? Put more succinctly, will Charlie get the dough?

This question also happens to coincide with Charlie's stated desire, which is to acquire at least a portion of that money. In essence, there is only one question that requires an answer in the third act.

And it is answered without doubt. Charlie does not gain custody of Raymond nor access to the badly needed money. However, he ends up with—you guessed it—"something better."

In this case, the something better is a "family." Recall that at the beginning of the movie, Charlie has been estranged from his father for years. And his mother is long dead. He has always believed that he was an only child. He surely isn't aware that he has an older brother in a mental hospital back in Ohio. In short, Charlie has no semblance of family when we first meet him.

Everyone needs a family, right? Or it sure is a nice thing to have, at the very least. And probably most of us would agree that you can't put a price on family. It's far better than money. And usually gives us greater satisfaction. From appearances, Charlie has (or had) money at the start of the film. But there is no doubt that it hasn't provided him with either happiness or peace.

At the end, Charlie eschews the money offered to him without strings by Doctor Bruner. But Charlie does not leave this film empty-handed, for he winds up with a "family," in the form of a brother he never knew he had. And with whom he has made a real connection. It is no leap in logic to suggest that Charlie has always wished he had more of a family connection. In fact, he even tells his girlfriend that he doesn't blame his father for cutting him out of his will. He would have done the same thing, he says. Leading us to believe that Charlie knows the importance of having a family bond. Which is what he eventually gets at the end.

Will Charlie's relationship with Raymond work out over the long run? Who knows for sure? But based on the "bridge" scene, we have hope that it will. Which means that Charlie has ended up with "something better" than the money he desired at the start.

(3) *Good Will Hunting*

The question raised at the end of the first act is what will happen to Will now that he has been forced by the court to meet with a psychotherapist and a math professor from MIT? Or, more simply, will he remain a genius janitor?

Recall also that Will's stated desire, as we learn late in the second act, is to remain in South Boston for the rest of his life with his buds who are, in essence, his surrogate family. Thus, we have two questions that need answering in this film.

In the third act, we get an answer to both. Will has a breakthrough and comes to grips with his past and its effect on his present life. In addition, we are also convinced that he will seek employment more in keeping with his considerable skills.

As for his stated desire to remain in South Boston with Chuck and the others, we get an unequivocal answer to that as well. Will leaves Sean (and us) a note to tell us his intention. He's going to see about a girl. All the way to California, far from South Boston.

Will doesn't get what he wants—to stay in Boston. He gets "something better"—a resolution of his past and an opportunity to form a real relationship and a possible family in the more traditional sense of that word.

Would Will getting to stay in South Boston be a good thing? No. Will's got bigger things on the horizon. The minute we see him solve that math puzzle we know that. And we suspect he does as well. Remember when Sean questions Will about why, of all the places he could have been a janitor, he chose to do so at MIT? The implication is clear. Will knows it is far better to maximize one's potential than to hide it. He is simply afraid to do so for fear he will lose his friends, the only family he has ever known. That is, until the end. When he clearly gets "something better."

(4) *It's a Wonderful Life*

This one's a bit trickier. At the end of the first act, the question we are faced with is, what has happened to George Bailey to put him in a crisis that requires the intervention of an angel? Or perhaps, will George overcome this current crisis and find a solution to his problem (finding that lost money)?

George Bailey's stated desire is different than the question raised at the end of the first act. (It is also the opposite of Will Hunting's.) He wants to get out of Bedford Falls, New York. He wants to see the world and build big buildings and not be stuck running the small Bailey Brothers Savings and Loan, which he views as a ball and chain, far beneath his talents. George is no genius, but he believes he has the potential to accomplish greater things.

At the end of the third act, we get a clear and unequivocal answer to the question raised at the end of the first act: facing arrest for the loss of the money belonging to the depositors of the Bailey Brothers Savings & Loan, George is saved by the generosity of those very depositors (the citizens of Bedford Falls) to whom he has been somewhat of a savior for the past twenty years or so.

But with that outcome of the final battle, does George get what he wanted? No. George remains "stuck" in Bedford Falls. But wait. Is it fair to say that George being "stuck" in Bedford Falls is "better" than exploring the world and expanding his career options?

We get our answer in the ending of the film. By staying, George achieves the humbling satisfaction of knowing that he had helped hundreds of Bedford Falls citizens who might have otherwise fallen victim to the penurious ways of Potter. That is why they come to George's rescue. In addition, over the course of those years "stuck" in Bedford Falls, George has earned the love of a beautiful woman, his wife, Mary. And together they have had three beautiful children whom he obviously loves.

Can a life of adventure and travel be better than the admiration and respect of an entire town, not to mention a loving family? We know the answer to that. And in the end, so does George.

One could argue (quite effectively) that George's stated desire is to find the money that Uncle Billy lost. Or at least to replace it. Absent either of those, he wants divine intervention. If that were all, then George gets exactly what he wants in the end. And, thus, we have a happy ending.

But I don't think the inclusion of George's lifelong desire to leave Bedford Falls was put into the story as filler. He even mentions it to Mary on the night of his crisis. He wants it for a longer time than he wants that money. Maybe even more so. Which is why I think the townspeople coming to his rescue is such a good ending and why I think George gets "something better." Without that earlier, strong desire on his part, the reward given him by the people of Bedford Falls would not have nearly as much meaning.

Obviously, "something better" is not an ending that fits all stories. Sometimes, it is not only acceptable but preferable that our main character achieve his/her stated desire. *Something About Mary* and countless other romantic comedies are a testament to that. And surely Rocky Balboa didn't need anything better than the self-respect and admiration of others, which he gained by lasting the desired fifteen rounds against Apollo Creed.

Even a somewhat "unhappy" ending would not necessarily be made better by giving the main character "something better." In *Saving Private Ryan*, Captain Miller gets what he desires: he saves Ryan. Obviously, it would be "better" if he lived in doing so. But the "something better" ending I have described is meant to be *instead of* not *in addition to* the main character's stated desire. Allowing Miller to live after saving Ryan is not better than saving Ryan. Saving is saving. His death is a consequence and, as we discussed, a reinforcement of the theme of sacrifice that permeates this film.

So how can you tell when a "something better" ending might work for you and your story?

Well, the first thing to look at is your main character's desire. Is it phrased in the negative? In other words, does your main character *not* want something? Rick in *Casablanca* does not want to get involved (the same as remaining neutral).

Another possibility is that your main character wants something that, while not illegal perhaps, is not necessarily a good thing. Charlie Babbitt kidnaps his older brother. Not really a crime. But he takes a clearly disabled individual away from the safe environment he has lived in for his entire adult life in order to get money. Not a good thing. You can't create a great ending by giving your main character the object of his desire when that desire would hurt others or not be in their own best interests.

One could argue that George Bailey's desire to get out of Bedford Falls and travel the world is not a bad thing. And surely it's not illegal. But even George knows that it is a selfish desire in the context of his life there. Why else would he allow his brother to go to college when he wants so desperately to do so himself? And why let his brother move to Buffalo with his new bride when George's turn to go to college comes around a second time?

George knows what will happen to the Bailey Brothers Savings and Loan if he leaves. And, more important, he knows what will happen to the good citizens of Bedford Falls if the Bailey Brothers Savings and Loan is not there as an alternative to Potter's bank.

Let's return to our discussion of the types of endings and the question of what type might best suit your story. To help you determine that, you will need to look at several things:

- What is the nature of your main character's desire?
- Does your main character's desire fly in the face of his/her best interest?
- Will permitting your main character to achieve his/her stated desire bring harm to others or themselves?
- Will giving your main character "something better" than their stated desire be convincing to the audience and your main character?
- If you have written a comedy, does the Hollywood ending (a notch above "happy") elevate the comedy in your story?
- If you have written a romantic comedy, does giving your main character the object of their desire bring about sufficient satisfaction for the audience?

- If you have written a drama, does an "unhappy" ending reinforce your theme while at the same time answering the question raised at the end of the first act (and, if applicable, your main character's desire)?
- Will giving your main character something less than their stated desire leave the audience unfulfilled?
- Can you give your main character less than their stated desire and still provide hope for them (and us)?
- Does the outcome of the final battle involve a death or deaths?
- Can you resolve your plot with an "unhappy" ending and still answer the question raised at the end of the first act?
- Can you resolve your plot with an "unhappy" ending and still satisfy your audience with that conclusion?

Chapter Twelve

Some Endings That Didn't Work

So far, we have looked at a number of films with "great" endings. Endings that "work." In this chapter, we will explore some recent and high-profile films that did not perform up to expectations. In each case, I believe we can trace their less-than-desired success, in large measure, to their endings.

In no particular order, they are:

(1) *Road to Perdition*—"The wrong villain."

It pains me somewhat to use this film because I did enjoy it a great deal and feel that it did not receive its proper due. At the same time, I believe it fell short of "greatness" and an examination of its third act and its "ending" may reveal why.

In this film, Tom Hanks plays Michael Sullivan, a hired killer and all-around enforcer for John Rooney, a powerful mob figure (and Sullivan's surrogate father) who runs the Irish rackets in downstate Illinois in 1931. Outside of his job, Sullivan appears to be just another hard-working family man, devoted to his wife Annie and their two sons, Peter and Michael, Jr. The boys are curious about what their dad does for Rooney, but know only that it is a secret best left unexplored.

Of course, this being a movie, it will be explored. One evening when Sullivan has to leave the house "for work," Michael, Jr. hides

under the back seat of the car and goes along to a meeting his
father has with Finn McGovern, the brother of a deceased member of the crime syndicate. Accompanying Sullivan is Rooney's
jealous and dangerous son, Connor. Neither of the two men
knows that Michael, Jr. has tagged along.

The meeting goes awry when Connor suddenly takes out his
gun and shoots McGovern, leading to an all-out gun battle won
by Sullivan and (to a lesser extent) Connor Rooney. This becomes
the inciting incident when Sullivan and Connor Rooney discover
that the shootout has been witnessed by Michael, Jr. who had
been watching through a window from outside.

Despite assurances from Sullivan to Connor Rooney that his
son will keep this event a secret, Michael, Jr. returns home one
afternoon to find his mother and brother slaughtered in their
home. At nearly the same time, Sullivan finds out he has been set
up by Connor Rooney to be killed by someone at another meeting
from which he (Sullivan) barely manages to escape. Sullivan
knows now that he and his family are in danger. He races home to
find Michael, Jr. and the bodies of his wife and youngest son.

Sullivan then takes young Michael and heads out of town to
save himself and his son. This is the first-act plot point. And the
question raised is whether Sullivan can protect his son (and himself) from Connor and John Rooney, who he knows had to have
either ordered the killing of his wife and son or been made aware
of it.

Sullivan and his son face a series of obstacles in the second act.
They first travel to Chicago, where Sullivan asks for protection and
a job from a Capone associate named Frank Nitti. Sullivan is turned
down flatly. He and Michael, Jr. must then avoid being killed by
Harlen Maguire (Jude Law), an assassin hired by Nitti on behalf of
the Rooneys. Maguire nearly gets them at a roadside diner, but they
manage to escape and throw him off their trail. They then proceed
to rob a number of the banks controlled by Rooney in an effort to
find out information that will help Sullivan understand why Connor killed McGovern back at that fateful meeting.

Doing so, Sullivan manages to attract the attention of the syndicate's accountant, from whom Sullivan seizes the books in a hotel-room raid. But in the process, Sullivan is wounded and nearly killed by Maguire, who has been following the accountant. However, Maguire is also shot and, presumably, left for dead. Sullivan then has to recover at the farm of an elderly childless couple where Michael, Jr. has driven them.

As he recovers, Sullivan goes over the books and learns that Connor has been skimming from his father's enterprise and obviously killed McGovern to cover it up. Sullivan then takes his son and returns to his hometown where he confronts John Rooney in the church basement to inform him of Connor's dealings.

In a bit of a surprise, John Rooney admits to knowing about his son's thievery and deceit, but says he will do nothing about it because of "blood." Rooney chooses to align himself with his real son over his surrogate son. Thus, Sullivan remains on his own, his life and that of his son still very much in danger. This is the second-act plot point.

The third act appears to shape up as one in which Sullivan will have to use his skills to kill his enemies before they can kill him. And he does. His first move is to wait in ambush for John Rooney late at night on a deserted street, following a regular meeting of the syndicate. Despite being outnumbered, Sullivan kills all of Rooney's associates and bodyguards. He saves Rooney for last and Rooney tells Sullivan he is glad it is him who will kill him. Sullivan quickly obliges.

Sullivan and his son then travel back to Chicago where Sullivan gets the blessing of Frank Nitti and the Chicago mob to kill Connor and put an end to the "war." Sullivan is told where Connor is hiding. With Nitti's backing, he is allowed to enter the hotel, board the elevator, and enter the room, where he finds Connor in the bathtub. Without an ounce of resistance, Sullivan shoots his adversary and leaves.

We next see father and son arrive at the beach where they are, it is presumed, going to stay for a while with Annie's sister. However, while Michael, Jr. plays with the dog on the beach, Sullivan is taken by surprise in the house by Maguire who has recovered and is waiting there for them.

Michael, Jr. hears the shot. He enters the room brandishing a gun that he aims at the assassin. Maguire tries to persuade young Michael to give up the gun. We can see Michael, Jr. try to will himself to shoot. And just as Maguire reaches for the gun, we hear a shot.

We then see that Sullivan has survived just long enough to pull the trigger on his own gun and kill Maguire so that his son won't have to. This satisfies Sullivan's internal desire that his son not grow up to be like him.

The denouement is young Michael returning to the elderly couple and the farm, accompanied by a voiceover in which Michael, Jr. tells us that when people ask him about his father and whether he was a killer, he replies that he was just his father.

So, how would you describe the "ending" of **Road to Perdition**?

Well, using our definition, it would be something like this: Sullivan protects his son but dies in the process, leaving his son to lead a life different from his own. This contains the outcome of the final battle (protects his son) and the denouement (dies in the process, leaving his son to lead a life different from his own).

You can probably already see the problem with this ending. No, it's not that Tom Hanks gets killed (again). It's that the final battle that takes place involves the wrong villain!

Certainly, the outcome of the final battle (Sullivan protects his son) answers the question raised at the end of the first act. But he does so against the wrong guy! Connor Rooney is Sullivan's nemesis! He is the one who killed his wife and son. He is the one who started the entire unraveling of his life by killing Finn McGovern at that meeting (the inciting incident). That event changed Sullivan's life irrevocably. All that's bad in Sullivan's life grows out of that action by Connor Rooney.

This creates in the mind of the viewer an additional desire for revenge. Which Sullivan does achieve, albeit in rather undramatic fashion. Why? Because in the film, Sullivan battles *Maguire* last. Maguire, while no doubt evil, has no emotional connection to Sullivan. Like him, he is hired muscle, a paid assassin. Killing is his job. Connor Rooney on the other hand destroyed Sullivan's family. He should be the person Sullivan faces one-on-one in the final battle.

One could argue that the final battle actually takes place in the hotel room with Rooney in the bathtub, and that everything after that is the denouement. But if that is so, then the final battle breaks a different rule in that the main character should face monumental odds against his nemesis. Instead, Sullivan is practically escorted into the hotel room where he shoots an unarmed and decidedly disadvantaged Connor Rooney. There is no sense of overcoming any great odds. To the contrary, it is almost a letdown.

Certainly, the notion that the father should pull the trigger instead of his son in the final battle is wise one. But it could have just as easily taken place at the end of a final battle involving Connor Rooney. Preferably, a Connor Rooney surrounded by bodyguards and foot soldiers so as to make Sullivan's task even more difficult. There was no need to bring back Maguire. All that was required to make this a memorable ending was a higher-pitched battle between Sullivan and Connor Rooney, with the same outcome as the one involving Maguire. The denouement in the film (Michael, Jr. returning to the elderly couple) would still work, and the theme that the voiceover reinforces would resonate just as well.

This all goes to show that even talented writers and/or filmmakers can make the wrong choice in creating their "ending." Something you may be able to avoid by following the principles set forth in this book.

(2) *Minority Report*—"Changing Questions"

This film is Steven Spielberg's self-described "noir" film, though it is also clearly a science fiction picture. Either way, it is a promising movie that ends badly.

Set in the future, Tom Cruise plays John Anderton, a Washington D.C. police detective in charge of the homicide division that just happens to have a controversial new way of solving murder cases—they arrest the perpetrators *before* they commit the crime, using the special skills of three "pre-cogs" who "see" the crimes before they occur. Anderton himself is a crime victim, having had his young son kidnapped from a public swimming pool years before, leading to Anderton getting divorced and facing a lonely life outside of his work. As a result of his personal experience, Anderton is a strong believer in the pre-cog unit.

The inciting incident presents a nice twist: the pre-cogs "see" a murder that is about to happen with Anderton as the would-be killer! The plot point at the end of act one is when Anderton escapes from his former colleagues and goes on the run, with the intention of proving himself not to be the killer before he can be arrested.

The question raised at the end of act one is simple: will Anderton be arrested for the killing before it occurs, like all the others "seen" by the pre-cogs? There are a couple of other questions that may be just as important: (1) will Anderton actually kill the person the pre-cogs "saw"? and/or (2) will the pre-cog system be proven to be flawed? It doesn't really matter which you choose or even if you choose all of them since the answer to all three of those questions would have to be answered once we get to the appointed time and place of the "killing" that has been "seen" by the pre-cogs.

In the second act, Anderton learns of the existence of a "minority report," which is something that's generated when one of the three pre-cogs "sees" different things than the other two. In addition to continually escaping his pursuers, Anderton also has to have his eyeballs surgically replaced so that he can get through the security system and back into the pre-cog unit where he can kidnap the pre-cog who generated the minority report. He does so, and together they manage to find their way to the scene of the "murder"—a hotel room.

Once there, Anderton finds pictures of his son along with other evidence that seems to suggest that Leo, the supposed murder victim "seen" by the pre-cogs, is the person who kidnapped Anderton's son. While Anderton tries to process this, Leo enters the room. As Anderton holds a gun on him, Leo "confesses." But Anderton does not kill him. Instead, he arrests him. Leo then proceeds to tell Anderton that he was put up to posing as the kidnapper of Anderton's son in exchange for favors from someone. Leo then brings about his own death in the hopes that whoever made that promise will still keep it. End of act two.

The problem?

All three questions raised at the end of the first act have been answered! Anderton does not get arrested prior to the killing! He does not kill the victim! And the pre-cog system is obviously flawed! And all of this takes place before we even start the third act!

Now it can be argued that there are new questions raised with this plot point. Namely, will Anderton get arrested in a more traditional fashion (after the crime)? In addition, will Anderton prove *to the others* that the system is flawed? (Remember, Leo does end up dead and the police don't know that Anderton did not kill him.) And, finally, will Anderton find out who made the promise to Leo and who has hidden the information about the minority reports?

These are all good questions. But they are *new* questions! Until we see Lamar (Anderton's mentor) kill Danny Whitworth (Colin Farrell) at the beginning of act three, we assume that Whitworth is Anderton's chief nemesis. Now, in the third act, we find that it is Lamar. The film then becomes about Anderton confronting and defeating Lamar. Which is okay, except we have watched almost two hours of this movie and only now are we being told that! It's a bit of a nice surprise, but it makes for a rather weak ending.

In short order after Whitworth's death, we see Anderton go to see his ex-wife with the pre-cog. Once there, he gets arrested and placed in some form of suspended animation facility where all "murderers" fingered by the pre-cogs are kept. But he's not there for long, for he is soon freed from the facility by his ex-wife. All of these events are the preparation for the final battle.

The final battle occurs when Anderton confronts Lamar at a benefit for him (Lamar), in a scene rather reminiscent of the one that occurs at the end of *The Fugitive*. Anderton then exposes Lamar to those at the event and, in a struggle for his gun, Lamar is killed. This is the outcome of the final battle, and it answers the questions raised at the end of the second act. However, as already noted, those are new questions.

The denouement proceeds to show us that the pre-cog unit has been dismantled, which makes perfect sense after what has occurred. Likewise, we see that the pre-cogs are no longer in Washington. Instead, they appear to live together in isolation in a cabin somewhere far from there. Finally, the last scene shows Anderton back with his ex-wife who is now pregnant and, presumably, no longer his *ex*-wife.

See any other problem with this ending?

This is a Hollywood ending! Tacked onto a noir film! Noir films do not end "happy"! Nor should this one.

I have always thought that this movie should end in the hotel room with Leo being the true kidnapper of Anderton's son. And Anderton should not kill him, but instead, arrest him and hold him while he waits for the police to arrive. No crime would be committed. Anderton would get closure on the disappearance of his son. And the pre-cog system would be revealed as flawed in a nice ironic twist. Which is what we often look for in noir films. Of course, scripts being organic, other changes would have had to have been made (somehow resolving the Lamar conspiracy sub-plot). But I believe that would have been far superior to the result that we got.

(3) *Cinderella Man*—"First Act–Third Act Disconnect"

The summer of 2005 brought us this film, based on the true-life story of boxer James Braddock. The movie was directed by Ron Howard and written (in part) by Akiva Goldsman, both Oscar winners for their work in *A Beautiful Mind*. In that film, real life did not hinder Howard and Goldsman. Unfortunately, in this one it did.

As with *Road to Perdition*, it is with some misgivings that I include this film in this chapter. I enjoyed most of it. But I was somewhat let down by the ending (outcome of the final battle and the denouement). While the overall experience was pleasurable, I feel that a slightly different ending might have made this film "great" and not just good.

When the film opens, Braddock is a heavyweight contender who shows a great deal of promise early in his boxing career. We then jump ahead a few years to the midst of the Great Depression and (eventually) learn that Braddock has lost all his money in the stock-market crash. Braddock is still fighting, though he shows little of that promise. In fact, he breaks his hand in an uninspiring bout and has his boxing license revoked (the inciting incident). Barely able to keep his family fed, Braddock is forced to go to work on the docks, when he can find it. He even has to go on welfare to keep his family fed and together under one roof.

Then, years after his last fight, he is given a chance to fill in for a boxer who gets hurt and has to back out of a fight against the number two contender in the heavyweight division.

With no time to train, Braddock somehow manages not only to survive in the ring, but to win the fight! (More on this later.) He then decides to train and keep on fighting. He proceeds to fight and win two more times before he is given the chance to fight

Max Baer, the world heavyweight champion, who is a dominating fighter and already killed two men in the ring. This is the second-act plot point.

Braddock is an underdog of **Rocky** proportions when he steps into the ring with Baer. And like his fictional counterpart, Braddock manages to last the full fifteen rounds. But unlike Rocky, Braddock wins the fight by decision. True story. And that's just one of the problems with the ending.

First, the question raised at the end of the first act is whether Braddock will be able to support his family through the Depression. Similar to **Minority Report**, that question pretty much gets answered by the end of the second act when Braddock has regained his status as a heavyweight contender and has paid off all of the family's debts.

Note that Braddock's stated desire is the same as the question raised at the end of the first act: to feed his family and keep them together. Thus, the fight with Baer is no longer about supporting his family. True, in the press conference before the fight, Braddock says he is fighting for "milk." But that's as far as the subject goes.

Second, the question to be answered in the Baer fight (the final battle) seems to be: will Braddock die in the ring like the two other fighters Baer has killed? The problem with this? Fighting Baer is not even a possibility until after he has fought the three previous fights, all of which take place in the second act. Thus, the notion of Braddock dying in the ring against Baer (or anyone else) is not even raised until late in the second act and again early in the third. Simply put, there is no connection between this question and the first act except that if Braddock dies he can't support his family. But if he doesn't fight Baer, there is no indication that they won't be fed or won't stay together. He's not being forced to fight Baer. It's a choice he freely makes.

The final battle (the fight with Baer) certainly pits the main character against his greatest obstacle. But Braddock never actually says what he wants by fighting Baer. We suspect that he wants to win, but he never really tells us that. Nor does he tell us why he wants to win even if he does. We are left to assume an answer to both of those questions. We simply don't know what he wants except to stay alive. Thus, the focus of the whole fight for the audience is whether he will stay alive.

There is some mention of how Braddock has become a hero to the poor folks who are struggling as he did during the Depression. And fighting for them might be sufficient motivation for Braddock. Except that he never says that is why he is doing it. Plus, this motivation does not relate back to the question raised at the end of the first act.

Compare this to **Rocky**, where Rocky told Adrian on the eve of the fight that he knew he couldn't win but only wanted to go the distance. So for the entire fight, we watch and wonder if he will be able to do so. The difference? In **Rocky**, him wanting to go the distance is his way of proving he is not just another bum from the neighborhood, which is his stated desire and one of the questions raised at the end of the first act. There is no such clear connection in **Cinderella Man**.

In addition, as mentioned earlier, Braddock wins by decision. Now, there is nothing inherently wrong with that. Except that in boxing, winning by decision is far less dramatic than winning by a knockout or even a TKO. But that's what happened historically and the filmmakers couldn't very well change that. Moreover, the filmmakers raise the suspicion immediately after the fight that, despite out-boxing Baer, Braddock might not win a judges' decision. The problem with this is that it is not set up at all prior to the fight. It is well known in boxing circles that a challenger almost never wins by decision against the reigning champ. It is widely believed that a challenger has to win by knockout. Had this been set up, we might have felt more tension after the final bell because we already know that Braddock has not died.

Finally, I think one of the biggest problems with the ending of this film is that, upon his return to boxing early in the second act, Braddock's first fight (against Corn Griffin) is, in many ways, more dramatic and produces a more unexpected result than the one with Baer. Think about it. Here is a fighter who has not trained at all and has been out of boxing for years because of a broken hand. He's given all of a day to prepare himself for the bout. And he knocks out the number two contender in the heavy-weight division! Now that's drama!

Except that in this movie it occurs in the second act and not in the third. All the more reason why the filmmakers needed to find another way to make the Baer fight more dramatic.

It is my contention that the filmmakers had to make the fight with Baer about something other than staying alive. Death is the risk Braddock faces in entering the ring. But *why* does he risk it? As mentioned, he says he is fighting for "milk." Had this concept been expanded a bit, it might have made for a more dramatic ending. The denouement tells us that Braddock bought a house for himself and his family with the winnings from the Baer fight. When the movie opens, Braddock and his family live in a nice house. Now I am not suggesting that the filmmakers should have made the fight about getting a house. But they could have made a connection. They could have said that *winning the fight* against Baer would mean to Braddock that he would not have to worry about feeding and housing his kids for a long time. He could have said that with a win would come certainty as to keeping a roof over their heads.

Earlier in the second act, May (his wife) questions Braddock about continuing to fight after the Griffin bout. She points out that they have enough money to pay their bills. But Braddock says that in nine months they will be back where they were before the Griffin fight. The filmmakers might have saved this line for the third act and the Baer fight so that we knew what was at stake. And it would have tied the question raised at the end of the first act with the final battle and its outcome.

Certainly, the filmmakers could not have changed the outcome of the final battle for historical reasons. Braddock wins by deci-sion, even though that is less dramatic than a knockout. No way around that. But if they had told us why winning was important to Braddock (not just fighting, but *winning*), we would have concentrated on that possible outcome instead of focusing almost entirely on whether he could stay alive. Again, **Cinderella Man** is a very good film. But the ending did not live up to all that preceded it. And that is why I believe the film was not received as well as Hollywood had hoped.

Here are a couple of other films with flawed endings and my reasoning behind that opinion. See if you agree.

(1) *AI*

Despite the efforts of two of the greatest directors of our time, this movie was not well received. In my mind, it was doomed from the start by the fact that the main character's desire could not be fulfilled in a satisfying manner. Remember what it was? A boy robot wants to become real so that his "mother" will love him. How the heck do you end that one?

The filmmakers gave it as good a resolution as they could by having the robot-boy believe that the re-created/cloned-for-a-day mom was real. Except that while that may be satisfying to the main character, it is not very satisfying to the audience. And that is who must be satisfied at the end.

(2) *Open Range*

I found this movie to have its merits for the better part of three acts. But then it launches into one of the longest denouements ever filmed, undoing much of the enjoyment and satisfaction it creates for almost two hours prior to those final, seemingly endless scenes.

As we have learned, one of the purposes of the denouement is to give the audience a chance to say goodbye. Except that in this film we couldn't say goodbye because the characters wouldn't leave! Compare the denouement in this movie to that in **Witness**. Watch both again from the outcome of the final battle. Then tell me which you prefer.

I am a firm believer in the notion that you can learn as much from a bad film as from a good one. I think the same applies to endings. Try this yourself with some of the films you didn't like. Examine their endings in the context of the structure set out in this book. My guess is that you will often find that something in the third act was the problem.

Chapter Thirteen

Controversial Endings

Every so often, a film will come along with an ending that causes controversy. In such an instance, the audience, or at least a large portion of it, is moved to debate. To take a side. To argue about the film and its ending long after seeing it. While there may be infinite possibilities as to the cause of controversy in a film, I can think of three different ways in which such a controversial ending may arise.

First, it may occur because the "ending" is provocative, meaning usually that the subject matter involves something about which people have disagreements *outside* of the theater. That is, the debate already exists about the subject matter separate from the film. Thus, when confronted with that subject matter on the screen, many in the audience may question its use or portrayal in the film. Examples of this would be the usual hot-button issues we face in everyday society, such as abortion, gun-control, the death penalty, and various forms of sexual behavior.

Second, an ending may be controversial simply because it is, well, shocking to the senses. Here the offense occurs not because of the subject matter or a debate that already exists outside of the theater, but rather, because some action that occurs at the end of the story is simply jarring or unsettling. Usually, we're talking about an act of violence or a serious crime, though it could also mean an ending in which justice is not served (think **Chinatown** or **Mystic River**). Not all in the audience will be shocked or offended by such an action or scene and, thus, a debate may arise as to the film's merits.

Finally, an ending can be considered controversial if it leads to a debate about what it means. In a case like this, the ending is susceptible to more than one interpretation. Therefore, people will take sides based upon their own individual belief as to the meaning of the ending. And the controversy occurs simply because there can be no agreement.

But merely because a film's ending is controversial, does that mean it is also "great"? Or does the fact that there is debate about the ending preclude it from being considered "great"? Does it have to be one or the other? That's what we will explore in this chapter.

Let me start by saying that, in my opinion, not all "controversial" endings are "great." By the same token, not all "great" endings create controversy. Controversy for the sake of controversy does not make good art. In any form. And certainly not in film.

It should not surprise you then to learn that I believe that a controversial ending can be "great." *But only if it fits the story the writer wishes to tell*. Controversy forced onto a story that does not call for that type of ending will ring false, and will only leave the audience feeling cheated. Or at the very least, unsatisfied.

Recalling the definition William Goldman has given regarding endings, a "controversial" ending is more likely to be considered "great" if it is still "satisfying" in some way. And, of course, it should also be "surprising," though that requirement is likely to be met simply by virtue of the controversy.

If you follow the teaching of Aristotle, then the controversial ending is more likely to be considered "great" if it can be viewed as "inevitable." Looking back on it, if what happens at the end has to occur exactly as it does, given all that precedes it, then controversy or not, it is likely to be "great." (As with the "surprising" requirement, Aristotle's recommendation that the ending also should be "unexpected" would seem to be fulfilled simply by virtue of the controversy.)

With all of that in mind, let's examine three recent films with "controversial" endings and, using the structure outlined in this book, see if you would call them "great."

(1) *Million Dollar Baby*

As everyone knows, this film was named Best Picture by the Academy of Motion Pictures Arts and Sciences in 2005. Clint Eastwood took home an Oscar as Best Director. Paul Haggis was nominated for his screenplay adaptation of two (at least) short stories from the collection written by F. X. Toole. And both Morgan Freeman and Hillary Swank were honored for their acting.

Of course, the controversy arising from this film comes from subject matter highlighted in the "ending." In particular, it comes from both the choice as to the final battle, as well as to its outcome, the latter being far more the culprit than the former in the eyes of many. Of course, we are talking about assisted suicide.

Before we get there, we could easily have a debate about something as simple as the main character. Namely, who is it? Who drives the story in *Million Dollar Baby*?

In terms of screen time (not to mention poster credit), the main character would seem to be Frankie (Clint Eastwood). However, Maggie (Hillary Swank) appears on the screen nearly as much as Frankie. In addition, Maggie appears to have a more clearly defined want, although it changes from act one to act three.

More specifically, when the film starts, Maggie wants desperately for Frankie to train her. Once he agrees to do so (first-act plot point), she wants to fight increasingly more talented fighters until she is given a title shot. Finally, after her debilitating injury occurs (second-act plot point), she wants to be freed from the misery of her physical condition, just like the dog she and her family had growing up.

Still, despite wanting so much, the fact that these "wants" change as the story progresses is reason enough to eliminate Maggie as our main character. Compare this to Frankie.

When the film opens, Frankie's want is to "protect his fighter." At that point in the story, his fighter happens to be a man named Willie, who hopes to fight for the heavyweight crown. Nevertheless, Frankie's "want" does not appear to be specific to Willie, as we learn over the course of the film from Scrap (Morgan Freeman). In fact, in Scrap's opinion, this desire on Frankie's part may be his fatal flaw as a boxing manager.

Thus, when Frankie agrees to train Maggie, we know that he will want to protect her just as much. In fact, he instructs her often that protecting herself is rule number one. But butting heads with this desire is Frankie's desire also to manage a champion. He never says so explicitly. But his actions tell us that this is a goal for him as well. This is Frankie's internal desire.

Everything considered, it would seem rather indisputable that Frankie is the main character in **Million Dollar Baby**. One could make the argument that this is a dual-protagonist film and I would not fight to the death over that. However, in dual-protagonist films, there is often still only one true main character and that is determined by looking at who makes the decisions involving both. Applying that standard here, there can be no question that Frankie would be the main character. Indeed, Maggie calls him "boss" and defers to him on almost every decision she has to make, from training to personal finance.

Moving on then, the question at the end of act one seems to be: will Frankie be able to protect Maggie and manage her to a shot at the championship at the same time? If that's too specific for you, then try this: what is going to happen now that Frankie has agreed to train Maggie (a girl) when we know that Frankie wants to protect his boxers, even to a fault?

As you know, we look to the final battle to get the answer to this question. And doing so, we already know the answer to the question at the second-act plot point (the injury). Frankie does not protect Maggie and she will never win the championship. So does that mean that the "ending" of **Million Dollar Baby** is not a "great" one?

To get the answer to that, we need to look a little closer. The outcome of the final battle is Maggie's death, assisted by Frankie. Which is where controversy comes in. Assisted suicide. Lots of heated opinion on both sides of the debate. There is no question that Frankie kills her. But what exactly does Frankie do and why?

First, it is important to point out that Maggie begs Frankie to kill her and, when he refuses, she tries several times to do so herself in the only way she can: by biting her tongue so that she might bleed to death. When that occurs, we're pretty certain that she is resolute in her desire to end her life. All doubt about her intention is eliminated.

It is important also to look at a conversation Frankie has with Scrap *after* Maggie asks Frankie to assist her in killing herself. In that discussion, Scrap tells Frankie, "Because of you, she got her shot." This is a crucial line because a shot at the championship is what Maggie wanted and, in part, what Frankie wanted for her as well. Scrap is telling Frankie (and us) that he has achieved his and Maggie's desire. All that's left now is "to protect her."

Recall that Frankie protects Willie right out of a title fight, as Scrap tells him. But it can be argued that Frankie does not protect Maggie when it matters: in that final fight against the Blue Bear. But while that may have been Maggie's last fight, it does not signal the end of the relationship between Maggie and Frankie. In fact, Frankie shows us that quite clearly. And he has one last chance to protect her. In this case, he can protect her from herself. And in the process, help her avoid any further suffering.

Remember that at an earlier point in the film, Scrap tells us that everything in boxing is backward. Frankie couldn't protect Maggie before or during the fight. But he can protect her now, *after* the fight. And he does so by assisting her in her fervent desire to end her suffering. Ultimately, Frankie gets what he wants. He gets his fighter a title shot. And he protects her in a far more important way than preventing her from getting her nose broken (as she did earlier in the film).

Now, this is not a "happy" ending. Nor is it a "Hollywood" or "up" ending. And I don't see anything "hopeful" in it. Certainly, Frankie does not get "something better." But in my view, it is the best ending for this film. If you disagree, then look at it this way: once the second-act plot point occurs, what other choice is there? To have Frankie abandon Maggie? To have him visit every day, but stand aside while she attempts to kill herself? The ending is inevitable. And unexpected. Just like Aristotle advised. And, in my opinion, that qualifies it as "great."

(One last note: notice that a death occurs as the outcome of the final battle. Note also that it is a "down" or "unhappy" ending. Just as we discussed in an earlier chapter.)

(2) *Lost in Translation*

You may not think of the word "controversial" when someone mentions this movie. But recall that one type of controversial ending involves that which is capable of more than one meaning, or at least one in which the meaning of the ending can be debated. Using that definition, *Lost in Translation* certainly qualifies. Of course, I am referring to the famous scene at the end where aging American movie star Bob Harris (Bill Murray) whispers something into the ear of young Charlotte (Scarlett Johansson) following their four-day "friendship" in Tokyo. Did I mention that we can't hear what Bob says to Charlotte? Ah, therein lies the debate.

But before we get to that, let's review the film briefly.

I think it is fair to say that this is a three-act story. I say that without knowing whether Sofia Coppola actually wrote the script with that structure in mind. Nevertheless, because the story is chronological in its telling, moving in linear fashion from beginning to middle to end, we can at least break it down into three acts.

Prior to discussing plot points and the third act's structure, it should be noted that this is a dual-protagonist film. Why do I say that? Well, Bob Harris and Charlotte have just about equal screen time, and they share what seems to be a similar, if not identical, want. I believe that can be best described as wanting to find meaning and/or comfort as displaced Americans in Tokyo for a week. In the case of Bob, he is there to film a commercial for Scotch whisky for a paycheck of $2 million dollars, instead of doing a play, as he tells Charlotte (and us) sheepishly. In the case of Charlotte, she is along on a business trip with her photographer husband who is less than attentive, leaving her to fend for herself almost the entire time. Note that the decision-making test does not reveal either one to be the main character because both make decisions about themselves and each other as a couple. Neither one dominates in this regard.

The inciting incident in this film occurs when Bob first sees Charlotte in the hotel elevator, though she does not notice him. The first-act plot point comes about twenty-three minutes later when they finally meet in the hotel bar and have their first conversation. Thus, the question raised at the end of the first act appears to be: will these two people develop a relationship that is something more than casual friendship? Or if you prefer: will they sleep together? Remember, both are looking for meaning and maybe a little comfort while staying in Tokyo, which is not quite the same as the question that is raised.

Once Charlotte's husband leaves Tokyo on a photo shoot early in the second act, Bob and Charlotte are free to spend time together. They "go native" with friends of Charlotte, sing karaoke, eat sushi, visit a Tokyo strip club, and watch Japanese television. And, of course, they talk. Over the course of doing all that, they seem to enjoy being with each other far more than they do with their respective spouses. This despite the nearly thirty-year difference in age. Which causes us to continue to wonder if something romantic will develop between them.

The second-act plot point occurs when Bob picks up the cabaret singer in the hotel bar and brings her back to his room where they spend the night. (You could say it happens some four or five minutes earlier when Bob decides to stay in Tokyo to appear on the talk show and I wouldn't argue too strenuously.) Charlotte knocks on Bob's door the next morning, and when he opens the door, Charlotte discovers what has obviously occurred the night before. This changes the story (and their relationship) and spins it in a new direction. However, the question raised at the end of the first act does not change. In fact, we wonder now if Bob's willingness to stray from his wife will lead him to Charlotte. And whether she will accept him now if he does.

In the setup of the final battle, Bob gets a phone call from his wife, Lydia, reminding him to be back in L.A. by Sunday for their daughter's recital. Charlotte and Bob then have a tense lunch at the sushi place, where Charlotte tells him, "Well, she [the cabaret singer] *is* closer to your age." Later that night, the fire alarm goes off in the hotel and Bob and Charlotte run into each other outside where they acknowledge their awful lunch. Bob informs her that he is leaving the next day, and she tells him she will miss him.

The "final battle" takes place thereafter. First, we see them together in the hotel bar where they first met. They hold hands. Bob tells her he doesn't want to leave. She tells him to stay there with her ("We'll start a jazz band"). At the end of the night, they end up in the elevator going back to their respective rooms. Bob says goodnight and kisses her awkwardly, twice, having missed the stop for his floor. They then each go back to their separate rooms, which is the outcome of the final battle. And the answer to the question raised at the end of the first act is: no, they will not take their relationship to a higher level than casual friendship. And no, they do not sleep with one another.

In the denouement that follows, Bob is downstairs the next morning and calls Charlotte's room to have her return the jacket that he has left there. Or so he claims. She doesn't answer because she's in the shower, and so he leaves a message.

Before Bob leaves the hotel, Charlotte comes down with the jacket, and they say another awkward goodbye. Charlotte leaves. And Bob gets in his chauffeured car to go to the airport. On the way, Bob sees Charlotte walking away on a busy street. He stops the car and runs after her.

When he catches up to Charlotte, they once again show the undeniable affection they had shown to one another before Bob's night with the singer. They hug for a long time, and then Bob leans in to whisper something in Charlotte's ear. Which is tantalizing because we can't hear what he says. Instead, they kiss and it is not the least bit awkward like the night before. Bob returns to the car for the drive back to the airport. Each is shown smiling. Finally, Bob utters the last word in the film: "Alright."

So why the controversy?

Well, naturally, everyone wants to know what Bob says to Charlotte! Actually, a good portion of the audience is perfectly happy with not knowing what he said. While another portion believes they should know this. Why is that? Presumably, those who wish to know think that whatever Bob says will explain why they did not take their relationship any further than simple friendship. Which may or may not be so. It depends on what he says. Moreover, regardless of what Bob says, there is no question that the relationship stopped at friendship. The outcome of the final battle doesn't change with the whisper. Those who don't care to know what was said are satisfied with that.

I maintain that those who want to know what Bob said are really asking for one of the elements of the third act's structure that I outlined in chapter 8. Namely, when Bob whispers in Charlotte's ear, we are being given a bridge scene. Almost, anyway. Remember, a bridge scene is one in which the main character "explains" why they are doing what they are about to do at the end of the film. In Bob's case, that is to get on a plane back to L.A. without having "consummated" their relationship. Except that Bob tells Charlotte the reason, but not us. Is that okay?

When I first saw the film, I did not think so. I thought it was cheating. I wanted to know. I thought I *deserved* to know after investing nearly a hundred minutes in the film. But just because I (and others) wanted to know, doesn't mean that we had a right to know in order to make this a "great ending." Frankly, if you think about it, what could Bob have said that would have adequately "explained" why they kept their relationship chaste? I know I would have had a terrible time trying to come up with something and probably would have failed miserably. For that reason, I believe that not knowing is okay and the ending still works, though we clearly have been teased.

That said, I also believe that the very same thing could have been accomplished without any whispering whatsoever. Bob chasing after and hugging and kissing Charlotte, without any words exchanged, would have accomplished the same feeling for me. By this time in the film, we know that they cannot take their relationship any further. It just wouldn't be right. Not from a moral standpoint so much as that it would have ruined the special friendship that they developed.

One final note: we said that Bob and Charlotte's shared "want" was to find meaning and/or comfort as displaced Americans in Tokyo. So did they ever get what they wanted? Without the scene on the street at the end, you might say no. But with them hugging and kissing, it is clear to me that they did indeed find both meaning and comfort. By finding one another. And forming their own special friendship. And by providing the answer to that question in the denouement, in my book, Ms. Coppola makes it a great ending.

(3) *Se7en*

The controversy arising out of the ending of this film can be summarized in a word: shock.

Unlike the previous two, *Se7en* does not tackle an issue about which there is debate outside the theater, nor does it have any ambiguity as to its meaning. Instead, this film delivers a body blow to the audience by completing the mystery in shocking fashion.

Before we get to the ending, let's look at some of the other aspects of the film.

For starters, this is a dual-protagonist film on the surface. Lieutenant Somerset (Morgan Freeman) and Detective Mills (Brad Pitt) share the screen equally. They even share the same desire (eventually) in that they want to solve and/or stop the serial killings, which involve the seven deadly sins. However, using the decision-making standard to determine the true main character, we would have to conclude that Somerset and not Mills is the main character. Until the very end, Mills defers to his mentor ("You're calling the shots, lieutenant").

When the film opens, Somerset wants to retire on schedule (in a week). Even after the murders begin, he wants to hand the case off to someone else, even suggesting to the captain that it be given to his replacement, Mills. But once Somerset accepts the dinner invitation at the home of Mills and his wife, Tracy (Gwyneth Paltrow), he becomes as fixated as Mills on stopping the crimes before the killer can rack up all seven deadly sins.

Our first-act plot point occurs just prior to this dinner when Somerset figures out that the killer intends to kill seven times, once for each deadly sin, meaning there are five more to come if they don't stop the killer. And that gives us the question raised at the end of the first act: will they catch the killer before he kills seven times?

Following three more killings and two brushes with the killer, the second-act plot point arrives when John Doe (Kevin Spacey) turns up at the police station with blood on his hands (literally) to turn himself in. This spins the action around because the police know of only five deaths, and they fear that they have missed or will miss the next two, even with the killer in custody.

The preparation for the final battle involves a series of scenes. In the first, we learn that the police don't know Doe's real identity or anything else about him. Thus, they have no direction in which to go to find these last two victims other than talking to Doe. Next, Doe's lawyer appears and offers a deal: Doe will reveal the location of victims six and seven and give a full confession, but only if Somerset and Mills accompany him alone to that location.

This is agreed to after the results of a forensics test reveal that there was blood from some unknown victim on Doe when he arrived at the police station.

Somerset and Mills then get fitted for wires so that they can communicate with the helicopters and police vehicles that will follow them to the location of the victims. They then escort Doe to the car in which they will drive to that location as directed by Doe.

The car ride is ten minutes long, mostly consisting of conversation in which Doe predicts the reaction of Mills and Somerset to what he is about to show them, along with those two policemen questioning Doe's insanity. The final battle begins when they arrive at the site with the burned-out trailer surrounded by all the power lines. One could argue that the car ride is the beginning of the final battle. However, I believe all of that conversation is really preparation and that everything that occurs after they get out of the car is the actual battle.

Once they exit the car, they walk out under the high-voltage wires into the open field where the victims supposedly are. As they do, a van appears on the horizon and drives toward them. Somerset goes to intercept it. When he confronts the driver, he learns that a package is being delivered to Mills. Somerset opens the package and finds that it contains Tracy's severed head (which we never see). At the same time, some fifty yards away, Doe tells Mills he has killed Tracy. It is clear from what he says that the box contains Tracy's head. Mills asks Somerset to confirm or deny this. Somerset does neither. Instead, he runs over to them to keep the now-distraught Mills from killing Doe.

Doe tells Mills the sixth murder victim was to represent "envy"—Doe envying Mills's "normal" life with Tracy. He then tells Mills that he wants him to kill him as this will complete the seven sins, as Doe's death at Mills's hand will represent "wrath." Mills obliges by emptying his gun into Doe, which is the outcome of the final battle.

There is a short denouement where we see Mills still in shock in the back of a squad car. Somerset tells the captain to do everything he can for Mills and that he (Somerset) is not going to retire ("I'll be around"). The film ends with a brief voiceover from Somerset in which he quotes Hemingway, saying, "The world is a fine place and worth fighting for." In the film's final words, Somerset tells us he agrees with the second part—which is why we assume he will not retire.

Of course, Gwyneth Paltrow's head in the box is our controversy. Not in itself. But in the fact that Doe completes his killing spree by taking the life of the wife of the detective who will then end Doe's life. This is surely not an ending for the faint of heart. Even though we never see Tracy's head in the box, we are shocked. We are shocked by both the severity of the crime, as well as by the fact that the ending is not a positive one.

Like **Million Dollar Baby**, this ending is not "happy," "Hollywood," or "hopeful." Somerset does not get "something better." Instead, we get just what we asked for: an answer to the question raised at the end of the first act. Remember what that was? Will they catch the killer before he completes his "masterpiece"? Well, the answer is no. True, they do kill him. But he has completed what he set out to do.

So does that mean it is not "great"? You be the judge. In my estimation, because this killer was so skilled and because they were never able to capture him (he turns himself in, remember), it is inevitable that he complete the crime before he dies. Given how many movies we've seen where the cops catch the bad guys before they can get away with everything, I guess you could say that it is also "unexpected."

And while it is surely "surprising," I don't believe many would say that this ending is "satisfying." By most people's definition, that requirement would have to mean that justice prevails. And that does not happen here. Much like **Chinatown**, another crime drama, we aren't necessarily comfortable with that.

In the DVD, director David Fincher describes an alternate ending the filmmakers considered in which Somerset (not Mills) fires the fatal shots into Doe. Same end result, but not a good choice. Why? Because in order for Doe's death to represent "wrath" he must be killed by someone who has the greatest need to seek vengeance. And that person is most definitely Mills, not Somerset. Were Somerset to kill Doe, we would get the same answer to our question. Doe would still complete seven murders. But having the wrathful sin be committed by the cop with less of a motivation to do so would not improve the ending in any way.

If you think that the filmed ending is not the best ending for this film then ask yourself how else this film could have ended and whether that would be satisfactory. Stopping Doe before the final killing (his) would only be satisfying if Tracy also does not die. And if Tracy does not die, then you need an entirely different third act. Which means an entirely different movie. And there is simply no way to know if that could be satisfying.

The lesson you should take from these three films is that controversy at the end of your story presents risk. On the other hand, you should not shy away from controversy if such an ending fits your story. And by fitting your story, I mean that it is both inevitable and unexpected. While some might disagree, if the ending is both, then it should also be satisfactory, regardless of whether it is also shocking, as in *Se7en*, offensive to some, as in *Million Dollar Baby*, or debatable, as in *Lost in Translation*.

Chapter Fourteen

Endings Outside of Three-Act Structure

So far, everything we have talked about with respect to endings has assumed that you are writing a screenplay involving a story told in three acts, with a single main character (or dual protagonists perhaps). And what I have provided is, in essence, a structure within a structure.

What about everything else?

You'll recall my rather unscientific breakdown of three-act movies versus those that are not, with eighty-five percent making up the former and fifteen percent the latter. That latter figure may be considerably lower than the former, but it is hardly insignificant. Not by a long stretch.

Those fifteen percent matter. They make up some of my favorite movies. Though you might assume otherwise, I love writers who break rules. We all do. But I hold firm in my belief that those numbers are not likely to flip-flop. They may vary within five percent from year to year or generation to generation. But we have been telling stories in three acts for centuries. It's built into our culture and, possibly, our DNA. It's not going away.

But neither are the rule breakers. And those rule-bending films all have to end. The screen will eventually fade to black and the lights will come up in the theater. And those "endings" must still "surprise and satisfy." That requirement is not restricted to three-act stories. Experience tells us that, does it not?

And if you choose someday to break the rules regarding structure, you will still seek what every writer seeks: a great ending. So how can you accomplish that outside of the three-act structure?

Well, it would be foolish of me to try to come up with "rules" for breaking rules. Not only wouldn't it work, but the results would not likely be "great."

Nevertheless, I believe that I can offer some general suggestions for coming up with endings for your nontraditional screenplays, and will attempt to do so in this chapter.

First, is there any way to categorize the fifteen percent of films that fall outside of three-act structure? Not in any comprehensive manner. Any attempt to categorize might be dangerously close to applying rules, which we all agree we don't want to do.

But I do believe that it might be helpful at least to break down that fifteen percent into two separate types of story, at least for the basis of this chapter.

They are:

(1) The multiprotagonist, event-based story; and
(2) all others outside the traditional three-act structure.

Multiprotagonist/Event-based Stories

These stories differ from those we have already discussed in that, as the name suggests, there is no single main character. For nearly all three-act films (true dual protagonists being the possible exception), there can only be one main character. We experience the movie through that one character. We learn of their desire and long to find out if they achieve it. In simplest terms, we put ourselves in their shoes.

In the multiprotagonist film, there are several characters, none of whom matter any more than the others because they all matter. They are joined by some common cause or desire. This cause or desire usually involves an event. Thus, instead of wondering about a character's desire, we wonder about the impact of the event upon these characters.

Note that these stories can be told in three acts. But they do not lend themselves to what we have talked about so far because the third act will not pit the main character against their greatest nemesis or obstacle, for obvious reasons. And any relation back to the first act will not involve a single character's desire, but rather how the event will shape the lives of the multiple characters.

A perfect example of this is **The Breakfast Club**. Instead of one main character, we have five equally important characters—three boys and two girls. Each of them represents a high-school arch-type, as relevant today as when this movie was made.

The event around which the story is based is Saturday morning detention in a suburban Chicago high school. Apart from getting through the day, there is no discernible desire for any character greater than any other. This does not mean that each of them lacks a desire. It's just that their individual desire does not propel the story forward from beginning to end. Instead, we watch because they all want to get through the day, and we want to see what happens to them when they do.

Another example is **Diner**. In this Barry Levinson classic, the event is the wedding of one of the six buddies. The intended groom has a desire: his bride-to-be must take and pass a sports trivia exam before the wedding. Likewise, each of the others have desires that are no doubt important to them. But there is no one single desire surpassing or outweighing the others'. Instead, we watch to see how everything turns out for them after the wedding.

Yet another example is **The Big Chill.** In this film, a group of friends from college gather for a weekend at the house of two of them following the funeral of one of the members of the group. Except for the obvious need to grieve their loss and to reminisce, there is no other common desire. One wishes to get pregnant. Another wishes to be taken seriously as an actor. Yet another wishes to maintain his reputation and standing in the community.

But there is no overriding desire on the part of any one member of the group. The event is simply the weekend reunion.

One of the advantages of this type of rule-breaking story (and what earns it a separate category) is that the event creates a natural "ending." Sunday will arrive, signaling the ending of the weekend in **The Big Chill**. So will the wedding in **Diner**. As will five o'clock Saturday afternoon in **The Breakfast Club**.

But merely having an event to help to conclude the story doesn't by itself help you create a great ending. It simply gives you a deadline. Something to shoot for. As in traditional three-act stories, you can (and should) still have surprises and reversals. And both of those things need some context. And context in this case means "character."

What tends to occur in these stories is that all, or at least most, of the characters come to some sort of realization or gain some new knowledge at the conclusion of the event. Whatever they believed or thought when the movie began, they now have more awareness or knowledge to add to or change those thoughts and beliefs.

Do not confuse this with "arc," which is the Hollywood term for when a character starts in one place psychologically, emotionally, and/or physically and ends up somewhere else that is decidedly more positive (think Rocky Balboa). The characters in multiprotagonist/event-based stories do not "arc" in the sense of some traditional three-act stories. That would be a lot to ask of a writer to create and for the audience to accept. Instead, they merely have a new understanding about themselves and, just as often, the others in the group. This new knowledge may lead to a change in their behavior in the future, though not necessarily. If this change in behavior occurs at all, we usually don't get to see it, although it may be hinted at when the movie concludes.

Going back to **The Breakfast Club**, you'll recall that when detention finally ends, each member of the group has had secrets exposed and/or truths revealed about themselves that leads to the others in the group seeing them in a different light. In some cases, as with Allison (Ally Sheedy), they are literally seen differently at the end. And with all of them, the experience of seeing the others in a new light causes them to view themselves with a different eye.

At the same time, this new understanding that each of them acquires over the course of the day does not lead to a change in the behavior of any of them. In fact, it is acknowledged that when Monday morning rolls around, they will not likely be friends or even exchange hellos in the hallway. Nevertheless, this ending is satisfying because high school is a universal experience and we know what is realistic and what is not when it comes to kids from different groups in school.

The same holds true in *The Big Chill*. When the weekend concludes, they all must return to their old lives. And but for the possibly pregnant Meg (Mary Kay Place), their lives will go on as before. But they all may view each other a little differently as a result of their weekend together. And by extension, they may regard themselves in a new light. If they share any common understanding after those forty-eight hours, it is that college is finally and completely over and a new more serious stage of their lives has begun, changing who they are.

A similar realization occurs in *Diner*. Though one of the group is already married when the film opens, the marriage of another represents a milestone. They can no longer be the same group of six as before. The previously married one has exhibited signs of struggle with his marital status throughout the film. But now that he will be joined by a second member, and maybe a third sometime soon, the group dynamic will change. This understanding is unavoidable following the time they spend together prior to the wedding.

You should note that multiprotagonist, event-based stories do not have Hollywood endings. Because there is no main character who is able to get exactly what they desire, there can be no miraculous outcome. For the same reason, "happy" endings as defined in chapter 10 are unlikely to occur. What you get instead is an "up" and/or "hopeful" ending, which is the natural consequence of gaining new knowledge or self-awareness.

And finally, because there is no single main character with a stated desire, this type of film does not lend itself to the "something better" ending.

Everything Else

How do you create a "great" ending for a story the likes of which we haven't seen before?

That's the objective of writing something outside of the three-act structure, is it not? To give the audience something that they haven't seen before?

No doubt. But the audience has experienced endings, both good and bad. And they prefer "good" if not "great." So when writing this type of film, the goal is no different. If anything, it is even more difficult. But that doesn't mean it can't be achieved or that one can't offer suggestions as to what to focus on to help create such an ending.

Before doing so, though, let's look at some of the ways writers have broken the rules from the standpoint of structure.

Over the years, we have seen films break rules with respect to chronology, telling stories backward in time (*Memento*) or in circular fashion (*Pulp Fiction*).

We have also experienced parallel stories (*Sliding Doors*) and alternative stories (*Run Lola Run*).

In each case, the things we have talked about in the prior chapters do not apply. And any story that chooses a similar path to those would require some degree of invention when attempting to craft a "great" ending.

Using the aforementioned films as illustration, *Memento* had to eventually end and did so by taking us back to the beginning. In doing so, the writer solved the mystery. In fact, a question is raised quite early in *Memento* that requires an answer at the end, not unlike a traditional three-act story. And we do receive such an answer. However, we don't get much in the way of a denouement because we have gone back in time and, therefore, have already seen the consequences of the ending on our main character. Indeed, the entire film can be considered the consequence.

In **Pulp Fiction**, we also return to the beginning at the end. The writers choose to end the story where it begins, disregarding the fact that one of the main characters in the final scene has died sometime earlier in the film. But the ending works because it shows us the transformation of one of the key characters in the film. The change in the character of Jules (Samuel L. Jackson) is key to the story and, because of one of the themes underlying this film, the diner scene provides a satisfying and surprising ending. The surprise is that this man who has made violence his vocation, chooses not to use violence to defuse the situation at the diner.

Sliding Doors concludes by having the two stories intersect and, eventually, resolve by taking only one path thereafter. This is both an inventive and satisfying choice by the writer. Other than in parallel stories, it is difficult to imagine how this ending could apply in any other circumstance.

Finally, **Run Lola Run** likewise makes a choice at the end, which seems inevitable because the main character cannot live all three alternatives in the same space and time. Like **Memento**, there is a clear question raised early on: how will Lola help her boyfriend recover the lost money? And an answer is just as clearly provided. But because much of the film involves scenarios that do not actually take place, one can hardly say that this is a product of three-act structure.

There are a number of other films like these that have their own unique endings, some satisfying and others not. Like the four just discussed, they have little in common.

So what can we divine about endings when looking at rule-breakers?

On the surface, not much. Your ending will have to work specifically for your story. There are no shortcuts. However, a closer examination reveals that some advice that applies to three-act structure applies here as well. Only more so.

Here are some suggestions:

- Surprise. You are breaking rules. The last thing you want to do at the end of your story is be predictable. Above all else, be sure to surprise your audience.
- Reverse. Aristotle suggested reversal of fortune in storytelling. It applies to film as well. Lead us to expect one thing and then give us something else (***Pulp Fiction***), while at the same time making it appear inevitable. Hard to accomplish, I know. But you are breaking rules.
- No loose ends. Just because you are telling your story outside of three-act structure doesn't mean you should violate this "rule." Loose ends leave audiences wanting and dissatisfied. You don't want that. And if you have raised a question early in your story, by all means answer it at the end!
- Resolve. Something. Anything. It's not necessarily "art" to simply end your story. We go to the movies seeking something different from our everyday lives. A resolution is one of those things we look for. So is the feeling of some kind of completion. As with endings in three-act stories, you don't need to resolve everything. But resolve something. If you don't believe me, take another look at ***Pulp Fiction*** and notice all the things that are resolved in that truly unique film.
- While doing or attempting to do all of the above, try also to bring your story around to a conclusion that reinforces a theme. This type of story tends to be more theme-based than traditional three-act stories. For that reason alone, you should try to nail your theme with your ending. It can be your signature for the film.

- If you are writing a multiprotagonist, event-based story, make certain that when you get to the end of the "event," your characters have transformed in some fashion. And, if possible, show us that they view not only the others, but themselves, in a new light as a result of experiencing that event.

The simple lesson here is, if you should someday choose to write a rule-breaking script, do not neglect the ending. The audience's desire to experience a "great ending" is no greater or smaller than in a traditional three-act story. It is the same. And, likewise, the overall reception of the script/film will depend heavily on how great your ending is, just as with any other film.

Conclusion

G reat movies have great endings. That's one of the reasons why they're great. Maybe *the* reason.

By the same token, movies that approach greatness, but fall short, often do so due to endings that don't live up to the rest of the film.

Every writer strives to create a great ending. The ending goes a long way in determining what emotion the audience feels when leaving the theater. More to the point, great endings can and often do leave a lasting impression in the minds of moviegoers. And as writers, isn't that what we are looking to deliver?

There is no "formula" for creating a great ending. If there were, they wouldn't be great. But as we have seen, there are certain elements that nearly all great endings share. And there is an order and structure that one can follow to help the writer create an ending to remember.

Having said all that, now comes a time for me to reveal something that I have not yet spoken about, mostly for fear that I might discourage you.

They change the ending all the time.

"They" means directors, producers, and sometimes even the actors. As you probably know by now, unless the writer is also the director (and has the very rare "final edit" provision in their deal with the studio), the finished film is not within the writer's control. Not by a long shot.

And driven by the need to make the most money (usually), filmmakers will consider a number of different endings for a movie. Many times, they will change the ending even at the last moment before release. (**Fatal Attraction** comes to mind here.)

Even in the average circumstance where money may not be the driving force, the ending may change from the writer's initial idea simply because the director (and/or producers) feel that it does not fit the rest of the story. As I mentioned earlier, **Saving Private Ryan** featured an ending in which Captain Miller survived the ordeal and walked away unscathed after saving Ryan.

And the ending of **American Beauty** was changed by director Sam Mendes from that originally written by Alan Ball, and in my opinion, the film would not have earned an Academy Award had Mendes not changed it.

So why do I tell you this?

Because it's true, for one thing. And because you should know it going in.

But also, it is to reinforce a notion that you may have overlooked or not given proper credence to. And that is that you have control over your ending at only one point in the process. And that point in time is when you submit the script to the decision makers. Once you sign a deal and accept their money, that power is relinquished.

With that in mind, you should *always* assume that they will leave your ending untouched. In fact, you should write your ending firmly convinced that they wouldn't dare touch it because it is the perfect ending for your story. In fact, it is a "great ending."

You can make it so and should. Before submitting your script, be certain that you have explored all the possible endings that might occur. Remember, the "ending" includes at least part of the denouement, so be sure not to give short shrift to that part of your script. Indeed, those words will be the last thing they read!

Under no circumstances should you submit your screenplay thinking that the "ending" is not that important because "they" will change it anyway. Nor should you submit your script hoping that "they" will be able to find a better way to give your story a "great ending." That's *your* job. Make it so they agree with you by giving them the best from the very start.

You have it within you to force their hand. Too many writers accept that the filmmakers can and often will change just about every aspect of their script, and they succumb to the temptation to give less than their best effort. To do so with the ending, in particular, can mean the difference between selling and not selling your script.

This does not mean that once "they" have purchased your script that you should block out every attempt they make to have you consider a different ending. At that point, you will have been paid for your script and will be considered a "writer for hire," both literally and from a legal standpoint.

As mentioned, both *Saving Private Ryan* and *American Beauty* were vastly improved by changes made by the filmmakers. In the case of Alan Ball, it earned him a gold statue. And for Robert Rodat, it meant a nomination and years of lucrative jobs.

You may ask why you should be so concerned about the ending at this stage if they and others benefited from filmmakers changing their endings? Well, as mentioned in chapter 2, *Saving Private Ryan* was based on an idea that is as good as I have heard in the last twenty years. It was going to get made regardless of how well Rodat wrote it (and he wrote it very well). And the rest of *American Beauty* was so novel and full of roles that actors would kill to play that it, too, was on its way to a green light from the moment it was purchased.

But you shouldn't count on that. As with the rest of your script, make the ending the best it can possibly be before you submit it. After that, let the development process unfold however it may. That, for the most part, is out of your control.

But that is then. This is the time where *you* are the "filmmaker." Always remember that you are the first to "see" your movie, and you have the power to make the reader "see" what you want them to see. So make them see a "great ending." One they will tell their friends about. One that will make you someone "they" will want to work with in the future. Because you will be known for delivering—you guessed it—a "great ending."

Appendix A

Thirty Questions

To help make sure that you write the best third act possible for your story, I am providing the following checklist.

If you haven't yet started your script, you may want to think about and answer many, if not all, of the questions below before you begin. Remember, you must know the outcome of your final battle (answer to the question raised at the end of the first act) prior to starting your script. You don't need to know your "ending" as I have defined it, because it includes all or part of the denouement and that portion of your third act may not become apparent until after you have started writing.

As for the remainder of the questions, you may not be able to answer each with specificity at this stage. But the more you can answer and the more specific you can be about that answer before you begin to write, the easier you will find the process.

If you have already written a draft or drafts and have doubts about your ending (or any other portion of the script), review each of the following questions and see what you come up with for answers. Doing so may help you to find any problems you might have with your script, and the answers you come up with may point you in the direction of a solution.

So here goes:

(1) Is your story one that can be told in three acts with a clearly defined beginning, middle, and end? If not, should it be?

(2) Can you reduce your story to a single sentence along the lines of "somebody wants something badly and goes after it against great odds"?

(3) Do you have a single main character who represents that "somebody"?

(4) If you have two main characters (dual protagonists), do they share a common desire or want? If not, then would it be preferable to make one of them the villain/antagonist?

(5) If you have two main characters (dual protagonists), does one of them make the majority of the decisions that drive the plot? If so, this is your main character. Write it that way.

(6) Does something happen to your main character prior to page twenty that changes his/her life irrevocably so that they cannot continue to live as they did prior to this incident?

(7) Does something happen after this incident, either as a consequence or as the main character's reaction thereto, that changes the direction of the story and sets the main character off on a literal or figurative journey?

(8) At the end of your first act, have you raised a question that the audience will look to have answered by the end of the third act? If not, can you go back and do so?

(9) Is the question that you raise at the end of the first act the same as your main character's stated or express desire? If not, keep this in mind when you come to the third act.

(10) As you enter the second act, does your main character face a series of obstacles that grow naturally out of the circumstances you created with your inciting incident and first-act plot point?

(11) Does each successive obstacle present a greater challenge than the one before it? If not, can you reorder them so that they do?

(12) Do you have at least three big challenges or obstacles that your main character must overcome in your second act?

(13) Does the last of those second-act obstacles lead your main character to a point in the story where the action turns around once again so that he/she must face the greatest challenge they have faced to date?

(14) Have you decided what that greatest challenge (the final battle) will be?

(15) Have you selected the time, place, and circumstances for that final battle? If so, have you made it so that the time, place, and circumstances place the main character at a decided disadvantage against whatever opposing force he/she must face?

(16) If you have a villain in human form in your story, have you arranged the final battle so that your main character will end up face-to-face with this character? If not, can you rearrange it so that such a confrontation will occur?

(17) Have you choreographed your final battle in such a way as to bring about the maximum dramatic effect from waging that battle? (Hint: look back at the main character's weakness and see if you can exploit that in this battle.)

(18) Do you have a clear outcome to your final battle?

(19) Does the outcome of your final battle answer the question you raised at the end of the first act?

(20) If your main character has an expressed or stated desire that is different than the question raised at the end of the first act, is that desire satisfied or resolved by the outcome of the final battle? (It may not be.)

(21) Do you have any subplots that have not been resolved at this point in your story? If so, can you come up with an action or exchange or a short scene or scenes that will resolve those unresolved subplots?

(22) Does the outcome of your final battle require or bring about a natural response by your main character? If so, what is it and can you show it?

(23) At the very end, does your main character act in a way that might cause the reader/audience to question why he/she is acting in that manner?

(24) If the answer to the previous question is yes, can you think of a "bridge" scene in which your main character can "explain" the motivation for the actions that are about to occur at the end?

(25) Does your main character have an internal or unexpressed desire or want that the reader/audience can perceive?

(26) If the answer to the previous question is yes, do you provide a resolution for or answer to that desire sometime prior to the end of the script?

(27) Describe the "ending" of your script to someone. When you do so, do you include in that description the outcome of the final battle and all or part of the denouement?

(28) If the answer to the previous question is no, can you rework the outcome of the final battle and your denouement so that the reader/audience has an answer to the question raised at the end of the first act, as well as a pretty good idea of what will become of the main character as a result of the outcome of the final battle?

(29) Does the type of ending you have chosen ("up," "Hollywood," "happy," "hopeful," or "down") correspond to the expressed desire of your main character?

(30) Might it make your ending better if you were to *not* give your main character what he/she wanted at the beginning of the story and give them something better instead?

Appendix B

Additional Resources

A s you no doubt already know, there are a number of books on the market about screenwriting. There are also several seminars and scads of instructional CDs and tapes, as well as a wide variety of web sites devoted to the art and business of screenwriting.

I am a firm believer in the notion that whatever you find that helps you to write your script is fine. If that means any one of the books that are out there, great. If it is your Aunt Mildred's Ouija board, then that's fine, too.

No one has cornered the market on screenwriting knowledge and understanding. Lots of folks have something to offer. It is my belief that if you can take even one thing out of any book you read that helps your writing, then it is worth whatever price you paid.

I believe also in continuing education. Screenwriting is no different than any other profession. Things change. Trends come and go. Old ways of doing things get abandoned and replaced by new methods. Doctors, lawyers, architects, and engineers all strive to keep abreast of changes in their profession. At least the good ones do. And that means continuing to learn about their profession on an ongoing basis.

With that in mind, I would like to offer some of the books, magazines, journals, and other resources I have read and learned from over the years. If you have not read some of these books, you may want to give them a look. It certainly can't hurt. And I would just about guarantee that you will gain some knowledge that you didn't have before from each and every one of them.

I have also included some web sites that I have found interesting and useful. Of course, not everything that appears on the internet is entirely trustworthy. There is no test that one has to pass in order to post something on the web. But the ones I mention here I have found to be informative and enlightening. I believe you will, too.

Books

Story, by Robert McKee
Regan Books, 1997, hardcover, 480 pages

Robert McKee has been offering his weekend seminar across the country for well more than a decade. This book sets out in written form the many principles he teaches in that seminar.

Screenplay: The Foundations of Screenwriting, by Syd Field
Dell, 1984, paperback, 272 pages

Most consider this to be the bible of screenwriting instruction. It certainly was the first of its kind, appearing in 1979, and is now in its third edition. Despite being more than twenty-five years old, I still use it in my introductory class at Boston College.

Screenwriting: The Sequence Approach, by Paul Joseph Gulino
Continuum, 2004, paperbook, 224 pages

As the title suggests, Gulino breaks down the screenplay into eight sequences, each making up fifteen pages of the script. While I do not use the sequence approach in my own writing, I do believe it is a useful way for other writers to tackle the rather imposing task of writing a hundred-plus-page script.

Making a Good Script Great by Linda Seger
Samuel French, 1994, paperback, 240 pages

Seger is generally credited with inventing the job of script consultant. This book is her best, in this author's opinion. Seger's instruction is easy to understand, and she uses simple examples to help illustrate her points.

The Tools of Screenwriting: A Writer's Guide to the Craft and Elements of a Screenplay, by David Howard and Edward Mabley
St. Martin's Griffin, 1995 reprint, paperback, 298 pages

This book contains a bounty of useful information for the aspiring screenwriter. Its principal author (Howard) is the founder of the graduate program in screenwriting at the University of Southern California.

Writing Screenplays That Sell, by Michael Hauge
Harper Resource, 1991, paperback, 325 pages

This book has also been around for some time, the first edition appearing in 1988. It is an easy-to-understand, general instruction book on screenwriting. Hauge's approach is similar to Field's and nowhere near as complex as McKee's.

Screenwriting 434, by Lew Hunter
Perigee, 2004 revised, paperback, 352 pages

Hunter is a screenwriting professor at UCLA. This book is his effort to put to paper the lessons he teaches at that school. He stresses simplicity in his approach to writing and offers useful exercises and advice.

The Writer's Journey, by Christopher Vogler
Michael Wiese Productions, 1998 (2nd edition), paperback, 360 pages

This book provides an easy to understand explanation of mythic structure and how it may apply to screenwriting.

The New Screenwriter Looks at the New Screenwriter, by William Froug
Silman-James Press, 1992, paperback, 369 pages

This book is a compilation of interviews with some very successful and talented screenwriters who offer their thoughts on the art and business of screenwriting. It is a follow-up to his earlier **The Screenwriter Looks at the Screenwriter**, which is also a good read.

Adventures in the Screen Trade, by William Goldman
Warner Books, 1989, paperback, 594 pages

This legendary screenwriter offers his thoughts and reflections on writing and movies. Full of great Hollywood stuff.

Magazines

While circulation may be down for magazines overall, screenwriters are fortunate to have three solid periodicals available to them. In alphabetical order, they are:

Creative Screenwriting

Fade In

Script

Published bimonthly, each of these offers the latest news about recent films, in-depth articles on various aspects of writing, as well as interviews from both new and established screenwriters. You could do a lot worse than to subscribe to one or all of these magazines in your effort to learn more about the art and business of screenwriting.

Web Sites

The Writers Guild of America (www.wga.org)

The official site of the Writers Guild of America, West. Lots of information for members and nonmembers about the current state of affairs in screenwriting. This site also provides links to many valuable sites of particular interest to screenwriters. The Writers Guild of America, East also has a site with some of the same useful information. I should note that Guild members who reside east of the Mississippi (like me) belong to the East, while those residing west of that demarcation point are members of the WGA West.

Wordplay/Fade In: (www.wordplayer.com)

This site was started and continues to be run by Terry Rossio and Ted Elliott, the writing team behind such films as *Aladdin*, *Shrek, Pirates of the Caribbean*, and *The Mask of Zorro*. Lots of columns about the various aspects of screenwriting that you won't find anywhere else. A real find.

Script City (www.scriptcity.net)

This site offers for sale screenplays for just about every film ever made. What makes these of value is that they come right from the producers of those films and, thus, from some stage in the development process. In most instances, these versions of the script will give you an insider's look into the evolutionary process that is filmmaking.

IMDb (www.imdb.com)

The world's biggest movie database (or so it says). Look up any movie, find the writer(s), actors, or key grip, if you wish. Great resource.

Box Office Mojo (www.boxofficemojo.com/daily/)

Daily, weekly, and monthly box office totals. And lots more. Every writer needs to know which movie made how much money.

Sources

Introduction

1. Syd Field, *Screenplay—The Foundations of Screenwriting*, Dell (1979)

Chapter One

1. Andrew Horton, *Writing the Character-Centered Screenplay*, University of California Press (1994)

2. Aristotle, *Poetics*, The University of Michigan Press (1967)

3. Alex Epstein, *Crafty Screenwriting*, Henry Holt (2002)

4. Kristin Thompson, *Story Telling in the New Hollywood*, Harvard University Press (1999)

5. William Goldman, *Adventures in the Screen Trade*, Warner (1983)

6. Michael Hauge, *Writing Screenplays That Sell*, Harper (1988)

7. Lew Hunter, *Screenwriting 434*, Berkley (1994)

8. Linda Seger, *Making a Good Script Great*, Samuel French (1987)

9. Robert McKee, *Story*, Harper (1997)

10. Syd Field, *Screenplay—The Foundations of Screenwriting*, Dell (1979)

11. Syd Field, *The Screenwriters Problem Solver*, Dell (1998)

Chapter Three

1. Linda Seger, *Making a Good Script Great*, Samuel French (1987)

2. Michael Hauge, *Writing Screenplays That Sell*, Harper (1988)

3. Lew Hunter, *Screenwriting 434*, Berkley (1994)

4. William Goldman, "The Best Medicine," *Premiere Magazine*, April (1999); *The Big Picture*, Applause (2000)

Chapter Six

1. William Goldman, "Rocking the Boat," *Premiere Magazine*, April (1998); *The Big Picture*, Applause (2000)

Chapter Ten

1. William Goldman, *Adventures in the Screen Trade*, Warner (1983)

Chapter Thirteen

1. William Goldman, *Adventures in the Screen Trade*, Warner (1983)

2. Aristotle, *Poetics*, The University of Michigan Press (1967)